Supporting the Professional Development of English Language Teachers

Applying the principles of facilitative teaching to mentorship, this book brings together well-established knowledge about mentoring with the experiences and ideas of mentors in the field to advance and support the professional development of language teachers. Recognizing the impact of globalization and technology, Smith and Lewis identify processes and pathways for mentors to develop multi-layered skills for working with teachers in both their own and cross-cultural contexts, and in face-to-face and virtual settings. Grounded in theory, this innovative approach is illustrated with authentic experiences, and ready to be applied by readers in their specific settings around the world.

With an interactive design that encourages participation and practice, each chapter includes vignettes, reflections, and challenging scenarios from mentors in training. Self-reflection and task sections at the end of each chapter engage the reader in combining theory with practice. Sample materials such as mentor-mentee contracts, work plans, journal templates, discussion suggestions (face-to-face or online), and observation forms deepen understanding and enable mentors to adapt or create their own materials. This practical and context-adaptable guide is accessible to mentors at any career stage, for use in personal professional development, or as part of mentor training sessions.

Melissa K. Smith is an Associate Professor in the School of Foreign Languages and Cultures at Ningxia University, China, and the founder of LEAPAsia, a non-government educational and teacher training organization.

Marilyn Lewis is an Honorary Research Fellow and a former Senior Lecturer at the University of Auckland, New Zealand.

Supporting the Professional Development of English Language Teachers

Facilitative Mentoring

Melissa K. Smith and Marilyn Lewis

NEW YORK AND LONDON

First published 2018
by Routledge
711 Third Avenue, New York, NY 10017

and by Routledge
2 Park Square, Milton Park, Abingdon, Oxon, OX14 4RN

Routledge is an imprint of the Taylor & Francis Group, an informa business

© 2018 Taylor & Francis

The right of Melissa K. Smith and Marilyn Lewis to be identified as authors of this work has been asserted by them in accordance with sections 77 and 78 of the Copyright, Designs and Patents Act 1988.

All rights reserved. No part of this book may be reprinted or reproduced or utilised in any form or by any electronic, mechanical, or other means, now known or hereafter invented, including photocopying and recording, or in any information storage or retrieval system, without permission in writing from the publishers.

Trademark notice: Product or corporate names may be trademarks or registered trademarks, and are used only for identification and explanation without intent to infringe.

Library of Congress Cataloging-in-Publication Data
A catalog record for this book has been requested

ISBN: 978-1-138-73527-9 (hbk)
ISBN: 978-1-138-73528-6 (pbk)
ISBN: 978-1-315-18661-0 (ebk)

Typeset in Bembo
by Apex CoVantage, LLC

To the mentors who lent their reflections and experiences to this book

Contents

Tables and Figures   ix
Preface   xi

SECTION I
Mentee-Centered Mentoring   1

1 Mentor and Mentee Identities   3
2 The Needs of Mentees   21
3 Setting Goals for Mentoring   38

SECTION II
Mentoring in Context   55

4 The Classroom Context   57
5 Broader Contexts of Mentoring   71

SECTION III
Interactive Mentoring   83

6 Challenges to Effective Communication   85
7 The Mentor's Feedback Role   95
8 The Mentor as Questioner   111

SECTION IV
Task-Based Mentoring — 125

  9 Classroom Observation — 127

 10 Group Mentoring — 150

 11 Action Research Projects — 165

     Conclusion — 183

     About the Authors — 187
     Index — 188

Tables and Figures

TABLES

p.1	Journal Entry Template	xviii
1.1	Mentor vs. Supervisor	4
1.2	Attitudes toward Mentoring	11
1.3	Mentoring Contract Template	17
1.4	Purpose Statement Template	18
2.1	Benchmarks Framework	25
2.2	Classroom Context Benchmarks	26
2.3	Needs Assessment Plan	35
3.1	Outcomes or Essential Questions	46
3.2	Mentoring Plan Template	48
3.3	Tracy's Mentoring Plan	49
3.4	Sarah and Steve's Mentoring Plan	50
5.1	Developing Self-Awareness	80
7.1	Conversation Openers	104
7.2	Interaction Analysis	108
8.1	Question Analysis	115
8.2	Fixed vs. Growth Mindsets in Mentoring Interactions	119
8.3	Encouraging a Growth Mindset	121
9.1	Observation Plan Template	141
9.2	The Story of a Classroom	143
9.3	Teacher vs. Student Talk Time	144
9.4	Managing Errors	145
9.5	Tracking Student Attention	146
9.6	Assessing Learning	147
9.7	Assessing Learning: Self-Observation	148
10.1	Advantages and Disadvantages of Group Settings	161

10.2	Group Task Plan Template	162
10.3	Peer Observation Form	163
11.1	Outcomes for a Mentoring Course	166
11.2	Qualitative and Quantitative Research	169
11.3	Article Template	179
11.4	Action Research Plan Template	180
c.1	The Story of a Mentoring Encounter	186

FIGURES

1.1	Complications and Possibilities for Online Mentoring	14
2.1	The Life Cycle of a Teacher	22
3.1	Learner Ownership Scale	48
4.1	Contexts of Teaching and Mentoring	59
6.1	Bloom's Taxonomy for Mentoring	89
7.1	Directive to Facilitative Feedback	99
7.2	Intervention Framework	100
7.3	Pragmatics for Feedback	105
8.1	Bloom's Taxonomy for Mentoring: Questions	113
10.1	Group Settings for Task-Based Mentoring	157

Preface

Reading experts sometimes like to remind us that reading, though a receptive skill, is not a passive process. Rather, it is an interaction between reader, text, and author. As you read this book, we invite you, the reader, to engage in this type of interaction. Not simply by invitation but also through the design of this book, we suggest that you interact with us, the authors, and our text, which includes ideas from other authors. As we share the experiences of mentors we've worked with over the years, you'll be interacting with them as well.

BACKGROUND TO THIS BOOK

In 2005, we crafted a blended distance and face-to-face program to train mentors working with expatriate and local English language teachers in Asia. The program covers two years and includes two courses in addition to an eighty-hour practicum. Ten years ago, we started with our first cohort. In 2017, we completed a journey with our fourth. Since the onset, we've worked with twenty-three mentors. They in turn have supported the professional development of numerous teachers, both expatriate and local, in various settings in Asia and the Middle East. At the same time, we've also continued to mentor teachers in our home and adopted countries and in Lithuania and India. Over the years as mentors of both teachers and mentors in these and other countries, we've learned as much as, or more than, we've offered. This book arises from those lessons.

We've often noted mentors' use of facilitative language teaching principles in order to support the professional development of teachers.

In part, they are mapping new experiences and knowledge about mentoring onto what they already know about language teaching. At the same time, language teaching principles simply make sound educational sense. Their insights have given us a new view of mentoring that has inspired this book. We combine the old (what is already known about mentoring language teachers as set forth in the existing literature) with the new (the experiences and ideas of mentors we've worked with), and we view them through the lens of language teaching principles. The result is an innovative approach to supporting the professional development of language teachers.

Our mentors have also inspired this book's interactive design:

1. Combining theory with practice;
2. Supported by examples, mostly made up of data from our mentors in training: their reflections, vignettes, and challenging scenarios (we've used this data with their permission and under pseudonyms of their choice);
3. Applied (by you) through self-reflection and tasks sections that you can complete for personal study or as part of mentor training sessions;
4. In both face-to-face and virtual, same and cross-cultural settings.

By the end of this book, you should be able to articulate your philosophy of mentoring, including your individual mentoring style supported by a rationale based on both theories and experiences (yours and those of other mentors).

READERS' BACKGROUND KNOWLEDGE

This book is written for language teaching mentors and those who train them. It can be used for personal professional development (by mentors) or as part of a mentor training session (by mentors and their trainers).

Whether you are a mentor or trainer, what do you bring to this book? First, you bring all your background knowledge. This includes your experiences as a mentor, for example, observing teachers and having conversations with them about the classroom, and what you've learned about mentoring from workshops, books, articles, and so forth. It also includes your experiences of being mentored, both good and bad. Memories of how nervous you felt when an observer visited your classroom, for instance, will deepen your understanding of affective factors and may influence your choices as you mentor.

IN THEIR OWN WORDS: ON BEING OBSERVED

Heidi reflects on her early experiences being observed, or in her words, supervised.

When I first began teaching and being observed by supervisors, I would put on the dog and pony show to demonstrate that I might know what I was doing. I felt the pressure of using the district/contract approved lesson plan form as well as the observation form. I was shooting for at least "Meets Expectations" but really wanted the "Exceeds Expectations" box to be ticked. There were times that I truly felt on the defensive. I am not quite sure when, but at some point, I gave a mental shrug and decided that they were going to see what I was planning to do that day without any coaching or prepping of my students. They were getting me, good/bad/mediocre day. As I could pick any class, I often picked my most challenging class of students to be observed. My reasoning was that I wanted help/suggestions for how to better engage that particular group. An outside set of new eyes to watch the class. I rarely ended up with more ideas from my supervisors. I learned more by observing other teachers myself.

Then there was the frequency issue for me. How is one visit a semester in one class session going to really inform my supervisor about my teaching? I preferred supervisors who wandered around campus and popped into my classroom unannounced to ask me a quick question or to just say hi. They saw what was happening at any given moment over a series of moments.

And I definitely fell into the camp that didn't like writing happening but also didn't like to see nothing being noted down. In the first case: What did I just do, and why are they noting it? In the second: How are they going to remember what I did to talk about it in a meaningful way? No winners there.

WHAT DO YOU THINK?

1. When you read about Heidi's experiences, what experiences of your own come to mind?
2. How are your experiences similar to or different from hers?
3. How might experiences like hers or yours influence the way that someone mentors?

You also bring your background knowledge about language teaching to this book. Your training and experiences in the classroom give you an understanding that is foundational to mentoring language teachers.

Moreover, because we view mentoring through the lens of language teaching principles, your knowledge of them will help you to understand this book.

HOW TO USE THIS BOOK

We hope you'll read this book and interact with it. In fact, we've included boxes like the ones above throughout the book in order to draw you into our *conversation*. Please feel free to spend some time simply reading and digesting what we have to say. But don't stop there. Instead, join the conversation by engaging in the following features, which you will find throughout each chapter:

1. **In Their Own Words** and **Here's What Happened**: Begin the process of application by reading **mentor reflections** and **vignettes** about the mentoring process.
2. **Puzzle It Out**: Go a step further and make decisions about what a mentor should do or what you would do in the **challenging scenarios** we share.
3. **What Do You Think?**: Take some time for **reflection** on chapter content or on "In Their Own Words," "Here's What Happened," or "Puzzle It Out" sections.
4. **Now It's Your Turn**: Finally, each chapter concludes with **tasks** you can do to help synthesize what you've learned and put it together into new and/or refined ways of mentoring.

As you join the conversation, one suggestion is to process ideas in either a mentoring journal or in regular conversations with other mentors, a mentor support group. See the tasks in "Now It's Your Turn" below for ideas about how to set these up. (Or trainers may have other ideas, like writing reflective papers or handing in some of the tasks as homework.)

WHAT DO WE MEAN BY *MENTORING*?

As we talk about how to support the professional development of language teachers, we've chosen to use the term *facilitative mentoring*. Before we can define this term, we first need to explain what we mean by **mentoring**.

In the field of TESOL (Teaching English to Speakers of Other Languages) today, supporting the professional development of language teachers is an ongoing concern not only for pre-service teachers in their practicum courses but also for in-service teachers in intensive English programs, adult education programs, private language institutes, both government and non-governmental organizations, and elementary through secondary schools.

One important aspect of professional development involves interactions between teachers and a more experienced practitioner who helps them decode the intricacies of teaching. Often this figuring out is viewed primarily as a series of classroom observations and follow-up feedback sessions. However, it also includes a variety of activities and interactions, one-on-one or in a group setting, that lead teachers toward professionalism—refined practices as well as self-evaluation and autonomy.

Some of the terms that are used to describe the interactive process of figuring out include *mentoring, coaching, giving advice, supporting*, and *consulting with*. In this book, we choose to use the word **mentoring** to describe the process whereby an experienced practitioner engages teachers in activities and conversations that support their professional development. We'll talk more about this terminology in Chapter 1.

WHAT IS FACILITATIVE MENTORING?

Now we come to the term *facilitative mentoring*. What do we mean? In *Advising and Supporting Teachers*, Randall and Thornton[1] view feedback on a continuum ranging from "authoritative" to "facilitative." In other words, advice to teachers can range "from directive mentoring (like directive teaching, explicitly telling a teacher what to do) to catalytic mentoring (leading a teacher to self-reflection, self-discovery, and self-monitoring)."[2]

We view mentoring, not only feedback, on a continuum ranging from directive to facilitative. While we believe (and will show) that there is a place for directive mentoring, we also believe that mentoring, by nature, most often occurs on the facilitative end, and it is this type of mentoring that will lead teachers toward the ultimate goal: "the ability to be self-evaluative and autonomous."[3]

Facilitative mentoring begins where teachers are and guides them toward where they need to be. Through facilitative mentoring, mentors support teachers' professional development not by directing them down particular paths but by negotiating paths with them, drawing on the knowledge and experiences of both mentors and teachers. Though this process may begin toward the directive end of the continuum, its goal is to lead toward the facilitative side, to a point where, without the help of a mentor, teachers reflect, self-evaluate, and enact decisions that have a positive impact on student learning.

OVERVIEW OF CONTENTS

In the sections of this book, four mentoring principles are elaborated on as a means of leading toward the facilitative end of the continuum.

Mentee-Centered Mentoring

Mentee-centered mentoring begins with identifying where individual mentees are and leading toward where each one needs to be. This process is accomplished within the context of relationships built on understandings of you and your mentees (Chapter 1). The process continues by identifying together their starting and continuing points (benchmarks) (Chapter 2) and then negotiating outcomes that lead them toward the ultimate goal: self-evaluation and autonomy (Chapter 3). "Now It's Your Turn" tasks in this section will help you, in collaboration with your mentees, to organize mentoring relationships, identify needs, and set goals.

Mentoring in Context

Helping your mentees reach goals would be difficult without an understanding of their teaching contexts. These include their classrooms and the dynamics of teacher-student relationships, roles, and responsibilities (Chapter 4). Mentoring in context also involves an awareness of differences in the broader context (of schools, systems, and cultures) and between your and your mentees' expectations and attitudes that may lead toward confusion or conflict (Chapter 5). "Now It's Your Turn" tasks in this section will encourage you, using your mentees as your primary informants, to deepen your understanding of their classroom dynamics and the influences of the broader context.

Interactive Mentoring

Much of what happens in a mentoring relationship plays out in conversations between mentor and mentee. Some of the complications you may face in these interactions include interference from an affective filter, the need to balance input and output, and differences between face-to-face and virtual communication (Chapter 6). Feedback is at the heart of interactive mentoring and is often considered a mentor's primary role (Chapter 7). Because questions are what characterize feedback interactions, honing your questioning skills is important (Chapter 8). In the "Now It's Your Turn" tasks in this section, you'll have an opportunity to analyze your mentoring conversations and make decisions about what interaction styles work best with your mentees.

Task-Based Mentoring

A mentoring task is an activity that engages mentees in learning about teaching. The most common of these tasks is classroom observation, which comes with its own set of issues and can be done in a variety of ways (Chapter 9). Although often seen as a one-on-one activity, task-based mentoring can also be done in groups, ranging from more to less formal setups, and can include both face-to-face and virtual elements (Chapter 10). Whether one-on-one or in a group, action research is another mentoring task that can lead toward reflection and refined classroom practices (Chapter 11). Each chapter in this section and the "Now It's Your Turn" tasks will take you through the steps of setting up and implementing mentoring tasks.

The conclusion will lead you back around to your professional development as a mentor. The culminating tasks will encourage you to take ownership of your growth as a mentor.

NOW IT'S YOUR TURN

Task p.1: Mentoring Journal

One way to interact with this book is to reflect on ideas in a mentoring journal. This journal can be in either a paper or digital format. If you choose this option, use the journal entry template in Table p.1 at the end of the chapter to get started. Feel free to adapt it to fit your style and needs.

Task p.2: Mentor Support Group

Another way to interact with this book is to process and reflect on ideas with a group of mentors or potential mentors. You can meet face-to-face or virtually. Once you've identified members, you'll need to choose a time to meet and a frequency (perhaps once a week or every other week for an hour) and a place or a mode (for example, a discussion board or forum, social media, or Skype). During your first meeting, you can decide on a schedule for reading, who will facilitate discussions and other activities each week, and how. Discussion leaders can draw on "What Do You Think?" and "Now It's Your Turn" sections in each chapter. The questions in the Journal Entry Template (Table p.1) may also be helpful.

Table p.1 **Journal Entry Template**

Date:	
Factual Summary:	Include here any information from the book that resonates with you (or perhaps from some of the sources cited in the book). It could be a general principle or idea, a quote, a summary of another mentor's experiences, a picture of a page or diagram, etc. If you are currently mentoring, you could also list information about the setting, situation, and teachers. Include any details and data that might help you remember the experience and learn from it or share it with others.
Reflections/ Insights:	Reflect more personally on your factual summary above. Some questions you might answer here are listed below: • How is my philosophy of mentoring developing? • How would I describe my mentoring style? • What am I learning about meeting the needs of my mentees? • What am I learning about mentoring cross-culturally? • What am I learning about mentoring face-to-face and/or virtually? • What principles or ideas have I seen at work in my mentoring experiences (as mentor or mentee)? • What approaches would I like to try with my mentees? Or which ones seem to work best with them? Which ones don't work well? Why? • How does this current experience compare to other mentoring experiences I've had? What patterns are emerging? • How well are the teachers responding to my mentoring? What should I try again? What should I change? • In addition to what the teachers are gaining from this experience, what other professional development experiences do these teachers need? What is something else from this book (or other sources) that I could try with them? • If I were going to advise a future mentor for these teachers, what would I suggest?

NOTES

1. Mick Randall and Barbara Thornton, *Advising and Supporting Teachers* (Cambridge: Cambridge University Press, 2001), 79.
2. Melissa K. Smith and Marilyn Lewis, "Toward Facilitative Mentoring and Catalytic Interventions," *ELT Journal* 69, no. 2 (2015): 141, https:/doi.org/10.1093/elt/ccu075.
3. Randall and Thornton, *Advising and Supporting Teachers*, 120.

REFERENCES

Randall, Mick and Barbara Thornton. *Advising and Supporting Teachers*. Cambridge: Cambridge University Press, 2001.

Smith, Melissa K. and Marilyn Lewis. "Toward Facilitative Mentoring and Catalytic Interventions." *ELT Journal* 69, no. 2 (2015): 140–150. https://doi.org/10.1093/elt/ccu075.

SECTION I
Mentee-Centered Mentoring

Mentoring includes the teaching of skills, of course, but moves beyond skill into perspective, motivation, and goals. Mentoring can change the entire direction of a life. I just can't imagine that occurring without the mentor and the pupil sharing a relationship that burgeons on genuine friendship.

—Asa

I began to be involved in teaching and mentoring years ago because I wanted to be able to make a difference in people's lives. I wanted to somehow make things better for them not by giving them something or doing something for them but by enabling them to make changes and do new things for themselves.

—Dom

CHAPTER 1

Mentor and Mentee Identities

WHAT DO YOU THINK?

1. What does the word *mentor* mean to you?
2. What type of relationship should a mentor build with a mentee?
3. What roles and responsibilities should a mentor fulfill?
4. Who are your (potential) mentees? What do you know about them as individuals, teachers, and mentees?
5. What potential challenges and advantages do you see to mentoring cross-culturally or in an online format?

Because mentoring as we define it below is a relationship, our discussion about mentee-centered mentoring begins with the identities of the two players in the process: you, the mentor, and your mentees. Then, in Chapters 2 and 3, you'll see how within that relationship you negotiate outcomes with your mentees based on their needs as you work toward particular benchmarks. At times, you may be leading your mentees from where they are to where they need to be, but often you walk alongside them and together head down the path toward teaching proficiency as well as autonomous learning.

This first chapter lays a foundation for the rest of the book. You will learn about the roles and responsibilities you fulfill and also begin to understand your mentees as individuals and teachers before identifying their specific needs in Chapter 2. Here, we also introduce two themes, cross-cultural and virtual mentoring, which are woven throughout the rest of the book. Most importantly, you will begin to organize your mentoring relationships.

HOW IS *MENTOR* DEFINED?

Different terms have been used to describe the process of engaging teachers in interactions and activities that lead toward teaching proficiency. The same is true of labels used for the experienced practitioner who supports teachers' professional development: *advisor*,[1] *coach*,[2] *supervisor*,[3] and *mentor*.[4] As Malderez[5] points out, there has been some "terminological confusion." Each term comes with its own definitions and connotations, which may change in different contexts.

HERE'S WHAT HAPPENED: MENTOR VS. SUPERVISOR

Some people taking a course on TESOL (Teaching English to Speakers of Other Languages) teacher mentoring were asked to reflect on different terms used to describe the relationship between a teacher and the person supporting her/his professional development. In particular, as they read the first few chapters in one textbook,[6] they focused on two labels: *mentor* and *supervisor*. Some of the words that came up in their reflections are listed in Table 1.1.

Table 1.1 Mentor vs. Supervisor

Mentor		Supervisor
elder	acceptance	judgment
guidance	help/helper	coldness
love	tender	critical
trust	balance	evaluation
truth	accountability	reporting
alongside	advice	weed out
constructive	wisdom	authoritative
together	edify	formal
understanding	available	negative
resources	modeling	checking
sharing	warm	top-down
friendly	pleasant	wrong
caring	two-way	standards
relationship		

WHAT DO YOU THINK?

1. What term is used in your context to describe the experienced practitioner who engages other teachers in activities and conversations that support their professional development?
2. What positive or negative connotations are suggested by the term?
3. What positive or negative connotations do the words *mentor* or *supervisor* suggest to you?
4. Which term(s) do you prefer? Why?

As the field's approaches to teacher learning have evolved, the term *supervisor*, one who assesses whether or not teaching is "done right," fits less and less.[7] In a facilitative approach where teachers are being led toward the autonomous learning of teaching, *mentor* seems to be more apt. However, because not everyone reading this book may see the term in a completely positive light, we need to explain what we mean.

WHAT MAKES A GOOD MENTOR?

Based on what others have said and the experiences of mentors we've worked with, the following sections describe the qualities of a mentor. As we define what we mean by the term *mentor*, you can begin to think about your own mentoring identity.

Relationship

In his "framework for evaluating mentoring quality," Arnold lists "establish [a] trusting and working relationship that lasts."[8] Although for the mentors in his study doing so seemed somewhat problematic, the ones we've worked with have found relationship to be a vital part of the mentoring process. To a large extent, they "experience mentoring as a relationship between themselves and their teachers."[9] In fact, many of them, like Asa in the forthcoming box, "can't imagine" mentoring without a relationship that "burgeons on . . . friendship."

IN THEIR OWN WORDS: A GENUINE FRIENDSHIP

Asa reflects on his experiences on both sides of the mentoring relationships.
There have been other more formal mentorships that I've participated in—sometimes as the mentor, sometimes as the pupil—and I find the same principle

> applies. I'm not a mentoring specialist, but it seems to me that a great deal of a mentor's role is to serve as a model for the pupil. Each of my self-selected mentors were people that I admired and, in some sense at least, desired to emulate. Of course, in more formal situations, where the mentorship is arranged, the mentor has to do the hard work of proving that they deserve to be emulated. This takes a while, and it requires the development of the same traits that are found (more organically) in informal mentorships: mutual trust, admiration, and enjoyment of one another's company. I just can't imagine wanting to be like someone that I didn't genuinely like as a person. I might admire a certain unlikeable individual's skills in a particular area, and I might even be able to learn certain skills from an unlikeable person, but mentoring goes far deeper than teaching a skill. Mentoring includes the teaching of skills, of course, but moves beyond skill into perspective, motivation, and goals. Mentoring can change the entire direction of a life. I just can't imagine that occurring without the mentor and the pupil sharing a relationship that burgeons on genuine friendship.

Figuring out what this relationship looks like may be complicated, especially because it may be different with every teacher mentored. Some of the paragraphs below may help, but first let's define it using the mentors' reflections in "Here's What Happened: Mentor vs. Supervisor" and "In Their Own Words: A Genuine Friendship." It seems that these mentors are looking to create, within a shared community, a relationship:

1. Of mutual trust, admiration, and enjoyment of each other's company;
2. Where an experienced practitioner comes alongside a teacher as a model and helper who edifies and offers wise advice in a way that is both caring and constructive;
3. That moves beyond skill into perspective and purpose and may flow over into life;
4. In which both mentor and mentee learn.

Everything we say throughout the rest of this section and the book will assume that mentoring is happening in the context of this type of relationship. At the same time, the paragraphs below elucidate more of what it looks like.

Roles

Within the context of a mentoring relationship, you may be expected to fulfill certain roles. We draw on ideas from our mentors to portray some of these roles and the tensions you may feel as you enact them.

Experienced Teacher

Exploring how English teachers in her Central Asian setting feel about being mentored, Sandra discovered that the word for *mentor* in their language can be translated "white beard." The way she summed up their ideas seems to express well the expectation many have: "How can you lead someone else down a road that you haven't been on yourself?"

Although mentors usually have more years of teaching experience than their mentees, that is not always the case. Instead, they may have a unique blend of experiences from a variety of teaching contexts (and possibly also life) that gives them something to offer. For example, some of the mentors we've worked with do not necessarily have more overall years in the classroom than their mentees. They do, however, have more experience teaching and living in a particular country and/or setting.

Expert Teacher

Because years of service does not necessarily equate with teaching proficiency, the sense that mentors are "white beards" is accompanied by the idea that they are experts in their classrooms and field. Many of the mentors we have worked with would hesitate to describe themselves as expert teachers. Instead, aware of both strengths and weaknesses, they are working toward building up the first while overcoming the second. Their teaching proficiency as well as their awareness, self-evaluation, and autonomous learning make them expert teachers.

Advisor

Randall and Thornton describe advice-giving as offering feedback in a supportive counselor-client setting that leads a mentee "to arrive at personally-derived plans for action."[10] However, they also use the term *critical friend*, which they fittingly call an "oxymoron."[11] In her reflections on a mentoring practicum, Simone expressed some of the tension she felt in her advice-giving role, wanting to be a "caring friend-like critical friend" and struggling to be "both friendly and professional."

Interpersonal Communicator

Good communication is central to the shared community of a mentoring relationship. Given tensions you may feel in your other roles, good communication may begin by tearing down walls of perceived inequality or a sense of threat. Like a counselor, you may need good listening skills, but as a critical friend you may also have to convey messages that are both pointed and palatable. Then, in certain settings, this role also includes intercultural communication skills.

Model

The first thought that may come to your mind here is "paragon of teaching." However, at least as important is modeling a learner attitude, reflective teaching, and autonomous learning. You may also be examples of how teachers can build a sense of community in their classrooms, manage the tensions inherent in giving advice to their students, and maintain good communication with them. In some cases, like the situations Asa described, this modeling may spill over into life.

Responsibilities

Much of what mentors do falls on a continuum, and the key to meeting your mentees' needs is to find appropriate points of balance in their particular contexts. Some of the continuums we and our mentors have worked through are explained below. Notice that the balance point is not necessarily in the middle.

Professional to Personal

On the professional end, mentors fulfill a "technical" role[12] in which they help mentees develop planning and teaching skills. On the personal end are issues of the heart that may include motivation, confidence, and anxiety.

To the mentors in our courses, mentoring is an interaction between the professional and personal. Accomplished within a genuine relationship, it is "a process of working with the whole person."[13] Understanding teachers' personalities, work and learning styles, aspects of their daily life, and even their "passions" is seen as a foundation for supporting their professional growth.[14] This may mean taking mentoring outside a professional setting and into more personal interactions over dinner or in an email. It occurs within the context of a shared community and "may involve putting one's whole self into the act of mentoring."[15]

Where should you aim to fall on this continuum? In this case, rather than either/or, the answer is both/and. Within the context of a genuine relationship, you can't have one without the other. The two sides are "inextricably intertwined."[16]

Directive to Facilitative

We mentioned this continuum in the introduction. Directive mentoring is like direct teaching. Mentors tell teachers what, how, and why.

Facilitative mentoring involves discovery learning, or an approach where teachers, with increasingly less help from their mentors, figure out the intricacies of the classroom on their own as they become autonomous.

Where should you fall on this continuum? While at times there may be a place for directive mentoring, the continuum is weighted toward the facilitative end. Allowing for cultural, personal, and other contextual differences, the facilitative end is, at least, what you should be headed toward.

Authority to Autonomy

This continuum is similar to the Directive to Facilitative one above. However, it presents the "dynamic tension between teachers' autonomy and [mentors'] authority."[17] In other words, it defines who has power to make decisions and take action in both the classroom and mentoring relationship.

Where should you fall on this continuum? Although different situations and individuals may require certain levels of authority, the continuum should be weighted toward the autonomy end. Given cultural and other contextual factors, you should, at least, be headed toward autonomy so as to empower teachers to take responsibility for their professional development.[18]

Evaluation to Development

At issue on this continuum is the primary purpose of a mentoring encounter. Regardless of who holds power, the perception of who does may be influenced by the overall purpose.[19] If the mentoring encounter ends with a report submitted to an administrator, teachers may see the mentor primarily as an evaluator. In many settings, this can add an element of fear or face-threat to the encounter and hamper the relationship.

Evaluation, like the training Richards and Farrell[20] discuss, may be focused on short-term goals and a pre-determined set of teaching skills. Development, on the other hand, starts with where teachers are and then, by reflecting on practice and exploring teaching knowledge, draws them further toward where they need to be. It is focused on long-term goals and "seeks to facilitate growth of teachers' understanding of teaching and themselves as teachers."[21]

Mentoring, as we define it, is facilitating a journey toward proficiency and autonomy as a teacher. It is developmental by nature. Ideally, you won't be submitting reports to a supervisor. However, the key to finding balance on this continuum may be figuring out how to approach the task, in spite of your mentees' perceptions (and possibly institutional expectations), in a way that promotes development.

WHAT IS MY MENTOR IDENTITY?

In our interactions with mentors in training, one of the most pressing questions they face, both from within themselves and sometimes from their mentees, is whether or not they are qualified or have the right to mentor. These thoughts are not specific to our mentors nor to ones of any level of experience or in any particular setting. In fact, an interesting study of experienced mentors across disciplines found that they viewed themselves "sometimes as novices and sometimes as experts."[22]

As you consider your mentor identity and face similar questions about your qualifications, remember this. How much experience you have may not matter as much as your unique blend of experiences, and your level of teaching proficiency is as important as your awareness and autonomous learning of teaching. Furthermore, in the same way that experience and expertise can be gained, mentoring skills can be learned. Interacting with this book is one way to develop your advice-giving and interpersonal/intercultural communication skills such that you become a better model of learning and teaching for your mentees.

Also remember that your identity is not fixed but dynamic. How you fulfill your roles and responsibilities changes as you learn and grow as a mentor. You also develop as you interact with your mentees and learn from them. In fact, you may not be able to figure out your mentor identity outside the context of a mentoring relationship.

WHO ARE MY MENTEES?

Figuring out your mentor identity and building a mentoring relationship are, of course, impossible without discerning who your mentees are. The next few chapters will go into more detail about identifying their needs and understanding their teaching contexts, but you can begin with the basics of who they are as individuals, teachers, and mentees.

Personal Characteristics

The process of understanding identities starts with the need to mentor the *whole person*. Before they are professionals, your mentees are cognitive, emotional, and spiritual beings. They have various personalities, work and learning styles, life stages and responsibilities, fears, and passions. Some are naturally reflective, self-evaluative, and autonomous. Other less so. Although in this book we categorize mentees by different characteristics, we also recognize that each one brings a unique blend to the mentoring relationship.

Expectations

A basic understanding of who your mentees are also includes their expectations of mentoring. How they view the relationship and your roles may be quite different from your ideas. Their thoughts about balance points on the continuums above may diverge from yours. Part of understanding the *whole person* is figuring out how much direction, authority, and evaluation they expect from you, if any at all.

Attitudes

Teachers' attitudes are also part of understanding their identities. In part, you will need to learn how they feel about the teaching profession and themselves as members of it. Some of our mentors in training have found that this is not always an easy process. For example, your mentees' feelings about their success in the classroom may not always parallel what you see. In other words, some people remain humble in the face of success, while others feel highly self-confident even when their performance needs polishing.

One of our mentors Ben used the term *buy-in* to describe a challenge he faced in setting up mentoring encounters with his colleagues. As he described the situation, his mentees lacked investment in the process. It is worth your time to consider and discuss with your teachers their attitudes toward mentoring. We present some potential attitudes in Table 1.2 below. Consider where your mentees fall and how you could pull them toward the left side and increase their *buy-in*.

Table 1.2 **Attitudes toward Mentoring**

Positive	Negative
This is great!	Whatever.
This will be fun.	This will be a chore.
I can't wait to get started.	I'm not sure I can handle this.
I have a lot to learn.	I've already learned enough.
I'll make time for it.	I'm too busy; it's an interruption.
I need it.	They forced me to sign up.
I sure could use some help.	Leave me alone.

WHAT DOES A CROSS-CULTURAL MENTORING RELATIONSHIP LOOK LIKE?

In addition to different attitudes and expectations, what complicates the mentoring relationship even more is crossing cultures. Although this is often a primary concern for non-native-speaking English language teachers, cross-cultural mentoring is much more than focusing on their language proficiency. Differences in perspective between a mentor, who may or may not be a native speaker of English, and mentee are what characterize cross-cultural mentoring. "In Their Own Words: Cross-Cultural Perspectives on *Mentor*" shows, for example, that the term itself (or whatever one is used) may imply different roles or responsibilities than you intend.

IN THEIR OWN WORDS: CROSS-CULTURAL PERSPECTIVES ON *MENTOR*

Anna reflects on the term *mentor* from the perspective of three cultures. In her reflection, she talks about her native culture and the culture within which she was living while addressing people from her adopted culture.

I was thinking a lot about the differences between supervisor and mentor and was trying to figure out why in my mind I've been personally leading toward supervision over mentoring as it applies in the field of teaching. Growing up in Eastern Europe, I had never heard of the term mentor until this term was borrowed from English just a few years back. Just a couple days ago, I double checked it in a dictionary and truly mentor is still literally translated as mentor into my native language. The term seems foreign in my language and culture. (Even though now, with various Western influences on my culture, it is becoming more and more popular!) When I think of an idea behind this term, friendship comes to my mind. And when I think about friendship relationships in my culture, I rarely think of true friendships between those who hold different statuses. Professional and personal relationships don't usually mix together. Work relationships are usually more formal, somewhat craving correction, supervision and evaluation.

As all of the above is simply my personal opinion, I did a survey among my Chinese colleagues to see what they think of the term mentor. With my limited Chinese, I asked about what this term conveys in Chinese. Below are a few of the responses I received:

A: *I would just think of it as someone who at university level has oversight for a postgraduate level dissertation and not much more besides. However,*

> *I think the English word* mentor *conveys more than feeling of one who provides guidance not merely academic but pastoral, holistic and long term.*
> **M**: *Mentor does: teaching students, learning strategies, assigning learning tasks, guiding and supervising students' learning process.*
> **R**: *When I think about the word mentor is giving someone help and advice especially for a long period of time.*
> **Q**: *Well, a mentor could be a person who can give proper teaching suggestions and has rich teaching experience, can also have useful strategies for dealing with students' problems effectively.*
> **G**: *Someone who is an expertise in his subject and is willing to help others. Maybe she can change a person.*
> **C**: *Not a lecturer or assessor, but effort a lot to give student learning support. Candidate can meet his or her mentor frequently, help learner to reflect his or her study. The mentor also may give further guidance.*

Individual mentees, influenced by societal norms, may have different expectations of your roles and responsibilities. Figuring out how best to relate to them may be complicated by cultural differences that require them, for example, to defer to someone in authority (which could include a mentor) or to devalue their abilities in order to show a socially appropriate sense of humility. They may also have a tendency to view themselves as *second-class* teachers because they are not native speakers. Above all, although we've presented cross-cultural mentoring as challenging and even problematic, as Anna's reflections have done for us, remember that it is a rich opportunity to expand your views of teachers, teaching, and the world.

WHAT DOES AN ONLINE MENTORING RELATIONSHIP LOOK LIKE?

When we first started thinking about virtual mentoring, it seemed full of complications until we remembered that from the first semester, our mentoring courses have included an element of online teaching, and it has worked. We've engaged in the virtual mentoring of our mentors. As technology has become more and more accessible, their opportunities for online mentoring have increased. In fact, just recently Steve had no choice but virtual mentoring, and what he discovered was a web

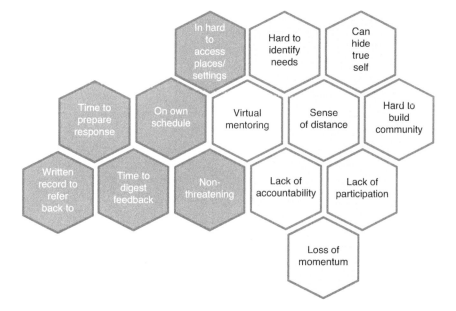

Figure 1.1 Complications and Possibilities for Online Mentoring

of both complications and possibilities for both mentor and mentee as illustrated in Figure 1.1. (You'll read more about his experiences with online mentoring in Chapter 6.)

What Steve experienced lines up well with the advantages and disadvantages Hall and Knox include in their survey of studies on language teacher education by distance.[23] What does this mean if you are trying to mentor in a virtual setting? There are both challenges and possibilities in doing so. You may have to work harder at building your mentoring relationships and managing participation. On the other hand, certain aspects may be easier in a non-threatening setting that brings in people from an interesting variety of contexts, all collaborating together as equals.

HOW IS A MENTORING RELATIONSHIP ORGANIZED?

In reflections after getting his mentoring program off the ground, Ben admitted that some of the challenges he faced were rooted in a lack of genuine relationship with his mentees. In fact, Ben seemed to connect the mentees lack of buy-in to his lack of investment in them. Like any relationship, one in a mentoring context works better with intentional cooperation.

In many ways, a mentoring relationship can develop naturally over time; however, there are also ways to support its growth. The tasks in

"Now It's Your Turn" will take you through some steps and encourage you and your mentees to negotiate three aspects of the relationship.

1. Practicalities: When, where, and how will you meet?
2. Purpose: What will the relationship look like, and why will you engage in it?
3. Personal: Who is your mentee, and how can you know each better?

NOW IT'S YOUR TURN

All of the tasks in this section are designed to help you organize a mentoring relationship. Task 1.1 is also set up as a topic for your mentoring journal or mentor support group. Tasks 1.2–1.4 assume that you are currently working with mentees. However, they could also be used as journal/support group activities. You could, for example, personalize (in your journal) or evaluate (in your support group) the Mentoring Contract Template in Task 1.2 and the Purpose Statement in Task 1.3.

Task 1.1: Defining *Mentor*

Step 1

Based on what you've read in this chapter (and what you've reflected on in your journal or discussed with your mentor support group), how would you define *mentor*? Write out a definition. Then, interview (face-to-face or virtually) a couple of potential mentees about their ideas. Some suggested questions are below.

1. What does the word *mentor* mean to you? Why?
2. How do you feel about being mentored?
3. (After sharing your definition of *mentor*) How does this definition compare to your ideas about *mentor*?
4. Does this definition fit better with a different term in your setting? What term?
5. How could this definition change your attitude toward being mentored?

Step 2

If you are mentoring in a cross-cultural setting, look up the word *mentor* in an English-local language dictionary. Then, interview two to three native speakers of the local language in order to find answers to the questions below.

1. What did you find out about *mentor* and how the term is used?
2. What connotations does *mentor* carry in the local language that are different from English?
3. Do you need to use a different word than what you found in the dictionary? Why?
4. What local language term works best to describe mentoring?

Step 3

In your mentoring journal, summarize and reflect on what you learn from your interviews. Or in your mentor support group, after members complete their interviews, compare ideas.

Task 1.2: A Mentoring Contract

Use the Mentoring Contract Template at the end of this chapter (Table 1.3) in order to lay a foundation for your mentoring relationship. You can adapt it to your particular setting and style. (For example, you could make it less formal by removing the signature section at the end.) This contract will be completed in stages:

1. Begin to negotiate practicalities with your mentee and complete the Schedule and Venue section now.
2. Task 1.3 below will help you to complete the Purpose Statement.
3. The Mentoring Plan will be completed in Chapter 3, Task 3.2.

Task 1.3: Purpose Statement

You and your mentee can use the Purpose Statement Template at the end of the chapter (Table 1.4) in order to compare and negotiate some of your expectations and decide on an overall direction for your relationship. As part of your discussion, you may want to summarize briefly some of the ideas you've learned in this chapter. You may also need to prepare more specific questions for each section in order to facilitate your negotiations. This purpose statement can then be used to complete part of your Mentoring Contract (Task 1.2).

Task 1.4: Who Are My Mentees?

As you negotiated with your mentee in order to complete Tasks 1.2 and 1.3, you likely learned quite a bit about each other's personal characteristics and attitudes toward mentoring. Consider what more you need to

Table 1.3 **Mentoring Contract Template**

Participants
Teacher:
Mentor:
Schedule and Venue of Meetings
Where, when, and how will you meet (face-to-face or in what virtual setting)?
Purpose Statement
What overall direction will your mentoring relationship take? (See Task 1.3.) Finish the sentence below. *This relationship exists to . . .*
Mentoring Plan
Attached to this contract is a mentoring plan negotiated between the participants and including details about what benchmarks are being aimed for. The plan also includes an overview of how outcomes will be reached or how essential questions will be answered. (See Task 3.2.)
Signatures
Teacher: _____   Mentor: _____ Date: _____   Date: _____

Table 1.4 **Purpose Statement Template**

	Mentee	Mentor
Defining terms	Compare your understandings of the terms mentor and mentoring? (This may be completed as part of Task 1.1.)	
Expectations	Compare your expectations.	
Relationship	What expectations do you have of the relationship?	
Roles	What expectations do you have of mentee and mentor roles?	
Responsibilities	What expectations do you have of a mentor's responsibilities?	
Purpose	What overall direction will your mentoring relationship take, and what roles/responsibilities will you each fulfill?	

know and how you could develop a shared community and perhaps a relationship that "burgeons on genuine friendship." Set up an informal interaction with your mentee in order to grow your relationship (possibly meeting for coffee/tea or a meal, participating in an activity or hobby you both enjoy, or connecting on social media).

NOTES

1. Mick Randall and Barbara Thornton, *Advising and Supporting Teachers* (Cambridge: Cambridge University Press, 2001).
2. Jack C. Richards and Thomas S. C. Farrell, *Professional Development for Language Teachers* (Cambridge: Cambridge University Press, 2005).
3. Kathleen M. Bailey, *Language Teacher Supervision* (Cambridge: Cambridge University Press, 2006), https:/doi.org/10.1017/CBO9780511667329.
4. Angi Malderez, "Mentoring," in *The Cambridge Guide to Second Language Teacher Education*, ed. Anne Burns and Jack C. Richards (Cambridge: Cambridge University Press, 2009), Kindle edition, chap. 26.
5. Ibid., 259.
6. Bailey, *Language Teacher Supervision*.
7. Malderez, *The Cambridge Guide*, chap. 26.
8. Ewen Arnold, "Assessing the Quality of Mentoring: Sinking or Learning to Swim," *ELT Journal* 60, no. 2 (2006): 119, https:/doi.org/10.1093/elt/cci098.
9. Melissa K. Smith and Marilyn Lewis, "The Language Teaching Practicum: Perspectives from Mentors," *The Teacher Trainer* 23, no. 2 (2009): 7.
10. Randall and Thornton, *Advising and Supporting Teachers*, 2.
11. Ibid., 23.
12. Ibid., 13.
13. Smith and Lewis, *The Teacher Trainer*, 7.
14. Ibid., 8.
15. Ibid., 7.
16. Ibid., 6.
17. Bailey, *Language Teacher Supervision*, 77.
18. Ibid., 75.
19. Randall and Thornton, *Advising and Supporting Teachers*, 10.
20. Richards and Farrell, *Professional Development for Language Teachers*.
21. Ibid., 4.
22. Lily Orland-Barak and Hayuta Yinon, "Sometimes a Novice and Sometimes an Expert: Mentors' Professional Expertise as Revealed through Their Stories of Critical Incidents," *Oxford Review of Education* 31, no. 4 (2005): 574, https:/doi.org/10.1080/03054980500355468.
23. David R. Hall and John S. Knox, "Language Teacher Education by Distance," in *The Cambridge Guide to Second Language Teacher Education*, ed. Anne Burns and Jack C. Richards (Cambridge: Cambridge University Press, 2009), Kindle edition, chap. 22.

REFERENCES

Arnold, Ewen. "Assessing the Quality of Mentoring: Sinking or Learning to Swim." *ELT Journal* 60, no. 2 (2006): 117–124. https:/doi.org/10.1093/elt/cci098.

Bailey, Kathleen M. *Language Teacher Supervision.* Cambridge: Cambridge University Press, 2006. https:/doi.org/10.1017/CBO9780511667329.

Hall, David R. and John S. Knox. "Language Teacher Education by Distance." In *The Cambridge Guide to Second Language Teacher Education*, edited by Anne Burns and Jack C. Richards, Chapter 22. Cambridge: Cambridge University Press, 2009. Kindle edition.

Malderez, Angi. "Mentoring." In *The Cambridge Guide to Second Language Teacher Education*, edited by Anne Burns and Jack C. Richards, Chapter 26. Cambridge: Cambridge University Press, 2009. Kindle edition.

Orland-Barak, Lily and Hayuta Yinon. "Sometimes a Novice and Sometimes an Expert: Mentors' Professional Expertise as Revealed through Their Stories of Critical Incidents." *Oxford Review of Education* 31, no. 4 (2005): 557–578. https:/doi.org/10.1080/03054980500355468.

Randall, Mick and Barbara Thornton. *Advising and Supporting Teachers.* Cambridge: Cambridge University Press, 2001.

Richards, Jack C. and Thomas S. C. Farrell. *Professional Development for Language Teachers.* Cambridge: Cambridge University Press, 2005.

Smith, Melissa K. and Marilyn Lewis. "The Language Teaching Practicum: Perspectives from Mentors." *The Teacher Trainer* 23, no. 2 (2009): 5–8.

CHAPTER 2

The Needs of Mentees

WHAT DO YOU THINK?

1. How would you describe your teaching proficiency? How would you describe your (potential) mentees' proficiency?
2. What growth is needed?
3. How could you determine needed growth?
4. How might standards or benchmarks help?
5. How does needed growth go beyond knowledge and skills?
6. How could you figure out exactly what help your (potential) mentees need?

Imagine a group of professionals lined up to participate in the sprint we call learning teaching. Some have an *inside track* with more knowledge, skill, teaching experience, or possibly even motivation than others. If everyone starts at the same point, teachers on the outside tracks are at a disadvantage, and this may exacerbate affective issues. Staggering starting points, on the other hand, is a way to meet needs.

The preceding chapter gave you an opportunity to lay a foundation for your mentoring relationships by understanding some of the personal characteristics of your mentees as well as their expectations and attitudes. This chapter provides you with a chance, in collaboration with them, to determine their teaching proficiency and identify needs. You'll be given some tools for ascertaining individual starting and continuing points, and you'll make decisions about how your mentees need to develop in order to run well because learning teaching is after all much more like a marathon than a sprint.

STARTING AND CONTINUING POINTS

One way to understand where teachers are in the growth process is to use a reference to determine points along the way toward proficiency. Some different reference tools are described below.

The Life Cycle of a Teacher

One useful tool is the life cycle model. Randall and Thornton's version,[1] illustrated in Figure 2.1, describes five stages of development that range from survival skills to expertise. The model suggests that teaching proficiency evolves from controlled processing to automaticity and at the same time from imitation to acting on intuition. The focus of a teacher's attention moves from self to learners and their needs, and planning becomes longer term. Moreover, initial react-in-the-moment strategies become routines for managing issues until the teacher is able to anticipate and solve problems before they occur.

The life cycle model is a tool you can use to determine your mentees' needs. To a certain extent, it also helps you focus on realistic expectations for them. As long as you keep in mind that each of your mentees will progress in unique ways, the model provides you with a broad view of their starting and continuing points.

Standards for Teachers

Although the life cycle model is helpful, using it to identify specific needs may present challenges because it deals in generalities. Standards can bridge this gap. They are a useful tool for determining the smaller steps toward each of the stages in the life cycle.

Recently the TESOL (Teaching English to Speakers of Other Languages) International Association has attempted to create and compile standards, primarily for the purpose of guiding teacher preparation programs

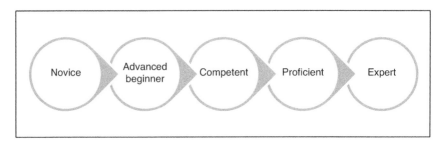

Figure 2.1 The Life Cycle of a Teacher

so that they know where they're headed (standards), "how to get there (the curriculum)," and when they've reached the destination (evaluation).[2] A different source, the Cambridge English Teaching Framework,[3] uses the term *competencies* rather than *standards* and is set up so that teachers can self-identify professional development needs and decide where to go next. You can find examples of standards on the websites of these two sources.

1. TESOL International's Advancing Excellence in English Language Teaching[4]
2. Cambridge English Teaching Framework.[5]

As you examine these standards, keep their primary purpose in mind. The "Standards for ESL/EFL Teachers of Adults"[6] envision their model with students at the core. No matter what tool you decide to use as a reference for your mentees, "student learning is the central concern."[7] This is what drives discussions about your mentees' needs. Also notice that the most common way of organizing standards is in domains or categories. For example, the "Standards for the Recognition of Initial TESOL Programs in P-12 ESL Teacher Education"[8] includes five domains: language, culture, instruction, assessment, and at the intersection of the other four, professionalism. Your mentees may have needs in some or all of these categories.

Standards may be a useful tool for identifying the needs of your mentees and then articulating outcomes to aim for. However, they also pose some challenges. As you look at the examples, also keep in mind the questions in "What Do You Think?" below. They are based in part on the potential challenges listed by Katz and Snow.[9]

WHAT DO YOU THINK?

1. How well do the domains cover teacher knowledge and skill, roles, and responsibilities?
2. How valid are the descriptions of different domains or standards?
3. How should teachers be supported to achieve them?
4. How should they be used, for development alone or also for assessment purposes?
5. How do we accommodate differences of opinion about what expertise looks like?
6. How well do the standards (and the domains they're presented in) fit with your (potential) mentees and their needs?
7. How could you use them to identify their needs?

An Exercise in Negotiating Benchmarks

As you look at the examples and answer the questions above, you may see both the benefits and the challenges in using standards to identify needs. That's what has happened as we've examined them with our mentors in training. This reference tool could make their job easier as long as we sort out some of the problems.

Terms

Chapter 1 described mentoring as developmental in nature. If standards are being used for evaluative or assessment purposes as in some of the examples above, they do not fit in a mentoring relationship. In order to address this potential problem, we've chosen to use the word *benchmarks* with our mentors because it comes across to us as more neutral. Rather than implying a level to be achieved or a model to be measured against, the term seems to indicate a frame of reference for deciding starting and continuing points and celebrating progress. Which of the two terms comes across as more neutral to you and your mentees?

Contexts

Another problem is that the domains and descriptions don't necessarily fit the contexts of the teachers our mentors work with. The solution has been to negotiate our own set of benchmarks. In the following paragraphs, you'll see some of the specific benchmarks we've come up with; however, we've only included a framework here in Table 2.1. Our main reason for this is that we want it to come across as an exercise in learning mentoring and not a set of benchmarks to use with your teachers. As our mentors have adapted standards to their settings, they've developed a clearer picture of how to help their mentees, and we think you would benefit from doing the same.

Types of Needs

Here's how the exercise worked with two groups of mentors in training. With the first cohort, we decided on four domains (theoretical base, contextual factors, instruction, and professional development), drawing on some of the categories in the standards for teachers referred to above. We also began to flesh out sub-categories. This is where the second cohort came in, further defining sub-categories and brainstorming benchmarks in each.

Table 2.1 **Benchmarks Framework**

		Knowledge	Skills	Affect	Values
1. Theoretical Base	The English language				
	Teaching				
	Second language acquisition				
2. Contextual Factors	Learners' culture(s)				
	Education climate(s) learners come from				
	Learners' first language(s)				
	Classroom context				
3. Instruction	Planning				
	Classroom management				
	Assessment				
4. Professional Development	Individual				
	Peer				
	With a mentor				

The domains, however, didn't seem to allow for mentoring the *whole person* (Chapter 1). As a solution, we envisioned our benchmarks in a two-dimensional framework. The domains make up the first dimension; the second describes their scope and is made up of four spheres. In other words, first teachers use head **knowledge** in order to understand within each domain, and then they physically enact that knowledge in the classroom through *skill* sets.

Our mentors have found that they can't easily separate the heart and soul from professional needs of their mentees. For example, sometimes in the process of learning teaching, attitudes interfere; sometimes strongly held beliefs make needed change difficult. Thus, in negotiation with our mentors, we added two spheres to the scope. The first deals with issues of the heart like motivation or buy-in, confidence and anxiety (discussed in Chapter 1). Expanding on this, the **affect** sphere consists of emotions and attitudes toward teaching, learners and their language and culture, language learning and teaching theories, and professional development.

Related but different enough to warrant its own category is the *values* sphere. Included here are teachers' beliefs that "are instrumental in shaping how they interpret what goes on in their classrooms."[10] In his book *Values in English Language Teaching*, Johnston, writing under the assumption that "all aspects of language teaching are imbued with values and moral meaning,"[11] says that "each teacher has a moral duty to examine her own values and beliefs about what is good and right for her own learners."[12] The *values* sphere gives our mentors a way, if needed, to encourage mentees toward a self-examination of beliefs and guiding moral principles that influence them in their profession.

An Illustration

Table 2.2 is an illustration of our exercise in negotiating benchmarks. What you see comes from domain 2: contextual factors, under the subheading: classroom context.

What's Next?

Another step with our next cohort of mentors, besides adapting and revising, might be to tease out benchmarks at each of the five life cycle stages or at each of the four levels on the Cambridge English Teaching Framework (from "foundation" to "expert").[13] You'll have an opportunity in "Now It's Your Turn" to engage in an exercise in negotiating benchmarks whether with your mentor support group or your mentees.

Table 2.2 **Classroom Context Benchmarks**

	Knowledge	Skills	Affect	Values
Classroom Context	• understand teacher and student roles • understand the cultural and social dynamics at work in interactions with and between students	• develop skills in investigating how culture impacts the classroom • display awareness of students' cultures and education backgrounds • manage teacher and student roles • help students develop intercultural communication skills	• increase their desire to learn about the cultural dynamics in a classroom • respect the students' expectations of the classroom context	• seek to understand student expectations rather than only to be understood • facilitate peace across cultures and between students

PUZZLE IT OUT: DISTANCE MENTORING IN THE MIDDLE EAST

Sarah and Steve are mentoring twenty Western teachers in the Middle East who teach in a variety of situations—children and adults, private and public schools and universities, and refugee programs. All the teachers have completed or are completing a TESOL certificate. In addition, some have education degrees (BA and/or MA). Their teaching experience ranges from none to a few years in their home or another country. A couple have taught for one to two years in their current country.

Within the larger group of teachers are two sub-groups. The first are teachers in their first one to two years of teaching. They are required by their company to take part in bi-weekly (every other week) professional development meetings in their locality under the guidance of a faculty coordinator. However, these meetings may or may not occur given the investment of the coordinator. The second group is these coordinators. In this case, Sarah and Steve are mentoring the mentors. For both groups, taking part in mentoring is based on their availability and willingness.

As Sarah and Steve consider options for mentoring, they have some obstacles to overcome. First, they live in one country while their mentees are spread out in three others. Identifying needs and mentoring can only occur in a virtual setting. Although they are well-equipped for the task with both a range of teaching experiences and training in mentoring, they have no experience in the particular countries and situations within which their mentees are teaching. Moreover, in addition to the voluntary nature of the current setup, as the semester begins, some of the mentees are faced with challenges that preclude them from full participation: teaching jobs that fall through, delayed visas, personal issues that distract them or take them back to their home countries, or feeling too busy to engage.

WHAT DO YOU THINK?

1. As you consider Sarah and Steve's situation, how would you describe the needs of the mentees?
2. Using one of the reference tools (the life cycle of a teacher, standards, or benchmarks), where are these teachers in the process of learning teaching?
3. What needs might they have in the *affect* and *values* spheres? How comfortable are you identifying needs in these two areas?

4. What more do you need to know (about the teachers or the reference tools) in order to determine their starting and continuing points?
5. How might an exercise in negotiating benchmarks expand your understanding of the reference tools?
6. How would you go about performing a needs analysis in order to gather necessary information?
7. In their setting, how important would it be for Sarah and Steve to identify needs in collaboration with their mentees?

NEEDS ASSESSMENT

Language teachers sometimes perform needs analyses, often informally, with the primary purpose of understanding what learners need in order to use language in their target contexts. Interactions with learners and other stakeholders about target needs subsequently shape decisions about outcomes and course and lesson design. For you, a needs analysis involves assessing where your mentees are in the life cycle or using standards or benchmarks as a reference by which to determine needed growth. It is a negotiation between stakeholders—teacher, mentor, learners, and sometimes also administrators—in order to identify what your mentees need in order to maneuver their target context (their classrooms) successfully.

When designing an English course for health-care workers, Uvin[14] discovered that performing a needs analysis before interacting with students in the classroom did not give a complete picture of their needs. For him, and for you with your mentees, cycles of needs analyses, before, during, and even after mentoring may be necessary. Identifying needs is an ongoing negotiation between stakeholders and in particular between you and your mentees.

The Mentee

The most important stakeholders in the process of learning teaching are your mentees. When you are performing a needs assessment, they are significant sources of information and also important participants in the process. Uvin found that when his learners did not play a role in needs analysis, they "could not always identify with the suggested content and methods."[15] Although time and situation may pose constraints, collaboratively identifying needs with your mentees gives them a personal investment in your mentoring. It increases their buy-in. This, in turn, gives them ownership of the process and encourages them toward autonomous learning. (We'll talk more about this in Chapter 3.)

From your perspective, when identifying needs in any of the spheres, you may have some concerns about coming across as pejorative. When you identify *affect* and particularly *values* needs, you may worry about imposing your principles on your mentees. However, collaborating with them relieves some of the discomfort, yours and theirs. When they self-identify needs, face threat is lessened and motivation to change increases. Moreover, an exercise in negotiating benchmarks with them allows you to use wording that fits their system of values.

Students of Teachers

Less obvious but still important stakeholders are the students who make up the target context. We noted earlier that learners and their needs are central to determining your mentees' starting and continuing points. Should you perform a needs analysis on their students too, then? Better yet would be to walk together with your mentees as they seek to understand their students and as a step toward identifying benchmarks. Needs assessment is after all part of the process of learning teaching.

Administrators or Supervisors

In certain settings, administrators may have a voice in your needs analysis. They may, first of all, have to grant permission before you begin mentoring. They may also play other roles. Although Asa set up a collaborative relationship with one of his mentees, benchmarks were, to a certain extent, determined by the forms he was required to complete for her practicum instructor. Another English language teacher in a public high school in the United States spoke about the mentoring agenda set up by district administrators. However, because mentoring is developmental rather than evaluative in nature, you should look for ways to collaborate with your mentees and, for example, choose benchmarks from within the fixed guidelines.

Mentors

Mentors are listed last here not because they are the least important but because they are the curators of everything collected from stakeholders. You are the one who may best be able to put all the information together or to see the big picture and then wisely choose which details to start with. Some ways you as curator could collect information from stakeholders are listed below.

1. Writing samples: With the permission of your mentees, these could include the following:
   - Their lesson plans;
   - Papers or blog posts they've completed for a course or professional development program;
   - Their philosophy of teaching written as part of their schooling or job search;
   - Students' homework, examinations, or questionnaires filled in for a needs analysis (assuming students' privacy is not violated).
2. Observations: Observations are, of course, a mentoring task. (See Chapter 9 for details.) They are also a means of understanding your mentees' target contexts and their needs. If an observation is not possible (whether in-person or virtually), consider asking your mentee's permission to read (and discuss with her/him) feedback or an observation report someone else has written.
3. Interviews or informal conversations: As you're setting up your mentoring relationship and collaboratively identifying needs with your mentees, interactions with them may happen naturally whether face-to-face or virtually. Getting permission from an administrator may require a formal conversation or email exchange in which you can also ask about guidelines. In addition, interacting with students may be an informative way to lay the groundwork for understanding your mentees' target contexts. (Section II will go into more detail about mentoring in context.)

IN THEIR OWN WORDS: MENTORING IN AN INTENSIVE ENGLISH PROGRAM

After a number of years teaching at a university in Asia, Anna and Ben were employed by an intensive English program at a university in the United States. Within their first semester, they looked for ways to be involved in mentoring. This was in part due to the need to complete an assignment for a course but also because of the value they have for professional development. In the paragraphs below, both of them reflect on the process of identifying needs.

Anna

We talked to our department head regarding any type of mentoring that would be purposeful here at our university and were told that we could guide some MA TESOL students in their program. The MA TESOL students are required to complete a certain number of observation and teaching hours. We could incorporate a blog for them. After sitting through my presentation at a TESOL conference (my topic was about mentoring in-service teachers), the department head expressed some interest regarding teacher mentoring, but that wouldn't start until January. Also, after talking to our colleagues, current teachers seem too busy for additional commitments. We are the new teachers here and are confused about what would be best for us to do.

Ben

After talking with many people, we have decided to go with a blog. We will be targeting MA TESOL students here. We have already had the chance to meet a few of these students as they have observed our classes and taught on behalf of our co-teachers in order to fulfill their own course requirements. Their teaching context here is a bit diverse, but 95% of our students come from Asia. The majority of those who will be following our blog also have their sights on overseas teaching, again mostly in the Asian context.

The group is not large and your questions (regarding how to engage teachers in professional development opportunities) are fitting. A couple of our colleagues who oversee this program have agreed to allow our blog to act as an extra credit assignment.

On top of the MA TESOL students, we will also be inviting teachers of ESL here at the university. They are very experienced and busy. I do not expect them to participate, but a little personal encouragement may help.

We are getting our blog up, will post the first discussion soon and send out invites. Let's see how it goes.

WHAT DO YOU THINK?

1. Anna and Ben have already started their needs analysis and have decided to set up a blog for MA TESOL students. How did they come to this decision? (How have they gone about their needs assessment so far?)
2. Where on the life cycle model might the potential readers of their blog be?

3. As you read their reflections, what needs of their mentees stand out? What benchmarks might they need to work toward?
4. As they make decisions about content for their blog posts and how to encourage discussion and participation, what further information might they need? How could they go about obtaining it?
5. What are some of the challenges they're facing?

GETTING STARTED ON YOUR NEEDS ANALYSIS

As you get started on your needs analysis, you may confront similar challenges to ones Anna and Ben or Sarah and Steve have faced in their mentoring settings.

A Reference Tool

For our mentors, none of the reference tools have seemed to suit their mentees. Or possibly they need to become more familiar with a tool before seeing how it fits. In either case, our exercise in negotiating benchmarks raised their awareness of the range of potential needs and made them more conversant in ones specific to their mentees. How might an exercise in negotiating benchmarks raise your awareness of mentee needs and increase your familiarity with the reference tools?

Whole Person Needs

For Anna and Ben, Sarah and Steve, *affect* needs, and in particular a lack of buy-in has potential to derail their efforts to mentor. They're hoping to encourage a value for professional development so that in spite of busyness each teacher opts in to mentoring. Including *affect* and *values* needs as part of our benchmarks framework has opened the door to looking for ways to encourage growth in these areas. What *whole person* needs do your (potential) mentees have? How could these needs be included in your reference tool?

Distance Mentoring

Identifying needs at a distance and virtual mentoring are not necessarily more challenging than face-to-face settings. Rather each comes with its own challenges. For Sarah and Steve, *affect* needs could be exacerbated by the ease of opting out when at a distance. Another challenge is a lack of experience in their mentees' particular settings and thus a need for deeper understanding. More collaboration (by email and Skype) and some virtual observations (see Chapter 9) offer a solution. If you are distance mentoring, what challenges are you facing in identifying needs, and what provides a solution?

Cross-Cultural Mentoring

One issue that may come up when mentoring cross-culturally (and sometimes across personal differences) is how much collaboration is expected by mentor and mentee. Some of our Western mentors working in Asian settings have struggled to encourage collaboration in identifying needs when their mentees defer to them as an expert or authority. The opposite can also pose a challenge when the mentor collaborates less than a teacher expects. Another issue is talking about *values* needs. For English language teachers no matter their cultural background, these issues may come too close to the taboo topics they teach their students to avoid. Yet, to others, a teacher's moral self is as important as knowledge and skills. (We'll expand on this in Chapters 4 and 5.) If you are mentoring cross-culturally, what challenges are you facing in identifying needs?

NOW IT'S YOUR TURN

The tasks below will help you deal with some of the challenges described above. In particular, they will encourage collaboration between you and your mentees. If you are not currently mentoring, Tasks 2.1 and 2.3 are designed as journal or support group topics/activities. You could also discuss terms for needs assessment (Task 2.2) with your support group or write in your journal about potential ways to perform a needs assessment (Task 2.4).

Task 2.1: Tools for Needs Assessment

Write about the following questions in your mentoring journal, or discuss them with your mentor support group.

1. Which of the reference tools for determining mentees' starting and continuing points seem most feasible to you (the life cycle model, standards, competencies, or benchmarks)?
2. Using the tool of your choice, how would you describe your own teaching proficiency?
3. How would you describe your (potential) mentee's proficiency?

Task 2.2: Terms for Needs Assessment

Interview a couple of your (potential) mentees in order to find out the information below:

1. What term (*standards, competencies, benchmarks,* or another term) works best to communicate a sense of development rather than evaluation?
2. If you are mentoring cross-culturally, what terms are used in the local language, and what connotations do they carry? Which term works best to express a sense of development?
3. When applying the chosen term to teachers and their needs, what categories might it encompass?
4. How comfortable are you and your mentees including *whole person* needs under this term?

Task 2.3: An Exercise in Negotiating Benchmarks

In your mentor support group, negotiate benchmarks (or whatever term you've chosen) that fit the classroom contexts of your (potential) mentees. Start with one of the standards documents referred to earlier or our benchmarks framework in Table 2.1. Then, adapt, modify, and create to come up with your own tool for determining starting and continuing points.

1. What domains seem to fit the classroom contexts of your mentees?
2. Do you also need a scope? What spheres will you include?
3. Will you incorporate *whole person* needs? How?
4. Where in your framework have your mentees already developed? In two or three of those areas, celebrate progress by articulating benchmarks they've already grown into.
5. Where in your framework might your mentees need to grow? In two or three of those areas, what's the next step? What specific benchmarks do they need to work toward?

Task 2.4: Needs Assessment Plan

Use the Needs Assessment Plan (Table 2.3) at the end of the chapter to make a plan for a needs assessment. It will help you answer the questions below.

1. How will you collaborate with your mentee in order to identify benchmarks? Task 2.2 may be a good starting point. You could also do Task 2.3 with them. What else would help you negotiate needs?

2. In addition to your mentee, who do you need to interact with?
3. What information do you need (from your mentee and other stakeholders)?
4. How could you obtain it (written samples, observations, interviews, informal conversations, etc.)? Will you use a face-to-face or online format?

Once you've obtained information from stakeholders, use the last row to list results—potential benchmarks to work toward with your mentee.

Table 2.3 **Needs Assessment Plan**

	Needs Assessment Plan		
	Mentee	Learners	Administrators
Information			
Collection Procedures			
Time and Location or Mode			
Potential Benchmarks			

NOTES

1. Mick Randall and Barbara Thornton, *Advising and Supporting Teachers* (Cambridge: Cambridge University Press, 2001).
2. Natalie Kuhlman and Božana Knežević, "The TESOL Guidelines for Developing EFL Professional Teaching Standards," TESOL International Association, accessed June 12, 2017, www.tesol.org/advance-the-field/standards/guidelines-developing-efl-professional-teaching-standards, 7.
3. "Cambridge English Teaching Framework," *Cambridge English*, accessed June 12, 2017, www.cambridgeenglish.org/teaching-english/cambridge-english-teaching-framework/.
4. "Advancing Excellence in English Language Teaching," TESOL.org, accessed June 12, 2017, www.tesol.org/advance-the-field/standards.
5. *Cambridge English*.
6. *Standards for ESL/EFL Teachers of Adults* (Alexandria, VA: TESOL International Association, 2008).
7. Kuhlman and Knežević, "The TESOL Guidelines," 6.
8. "Standards for the Recognition of Initial TESOL Programs in P-12 ESL Teacher Education," TESOL International Association, 2010, accessed June 12, 2017, www.tesol.org/docs/default-source/advocacy/the-revised-tesol-ncate-standards-for-the-recognition-of-initial-tesol-programs-in-p-12-esl-teacher-education-(2010-pdf).pdf?sfvrsn=4.
9. Anne Katz and Marguerite Ann Snow, "Standards and Second Language Teacher Education," in *The Cambridge Guide to Second Language Teacher Education*, ed. Anne Burns and Jack C. Richards (Cambridge: Cambridge University Press, 2009), Kindle edition, chap. 7.
10. Donald Freeman and Karen E. Johnson, "Reconceptualizing the Knowledge-Base of Language Teacher Education," *TESOL Quarterly* 32, no. 3 (1998): 401, https://doi.org/10.2307/3588114.
11. Bill Johnston, *Values in English Language Teaching* (Mahwah, NJ: Lawrence Erlbaum Associates Publishers, 2003), Kindle edition, preface.
12. Ibid., chap. 7.
13. *Cambridge English*.
14. Johan Uvin, "Designing Workplace ESOL Courses for Chinese Health-Care Workers at a Boston Nursing Home," in *Teachers as Course Developers*, ed. Kathleen Graves (Cambridge: Cambridge University Press, 1996): 39–62.
15. Ibid., 44.

REFERENCES

"Advancing Excellence in English Language Teaching." TESOL.org. Accessed June 12, 2017. www.tesol.org/advance-the-field/standards.

"Cambridge English Teaching Framework." *Cambridge English*. Accessed June 12, 2017. www.cambridgeenglish.org/teaching-english/cambridge-english-teaching-framework/.

Freeman, Donald and Karen E. Johnson. "Reconceptualizing the Knowledge-Base of Language Teacher Education." *TESOL Quarterly* 32, no. 3 (1998): 397–417. https://doi.org/10.2307/3588114.

Johnston, Bill. *Values in English Language Teaching*. Mahwah, NJ: Lawrence Erlbaum Associates Publishers, 2003. Kindle edition.

Katz, Anne and Marguerite Ann Snow. "Standards and Second Language Teacher Education." In *The Cambridge Guide to Second Language Teacher Education*, edited by Anne Burns and Jack C. Richards, Chapter 7. Cambridge: Cambridge University Press, 2009. Kindle edition.

Kuhlman, Natalie and Božana Knežević. "The TESOL Guidelines for Developing EFL Professional Teaching Standards." TESOL International Association. Accessed June 12, 2017. www.tesol.org/advance-the-field/standards/guidelines-developing-efl-professional-teaching-standards.

Randall, Mick and Barbara Thornton. *Advising and Supporting Teachers*. Cambridge: Cambridge University Press, 2001.

Standards for ESL/EFL Teachers of Adults. Alexandria, VA: TESOL International Association, 2008.

"Standards for the Recognition of Initial TESOL Programs in P-12 ESL Teacher Education." TESOL International Association, 2010. Accessed June 12, 2017. www.tesol.org/docs/default-source/advocacy/the-revised-tesol-ncate-standards-for-the-recognition-of-initial-tesol-programs-in-p-12-esl-teacher-education-(2010-pdf).pdf?sfvrsn=4.

Uvin, Johan. "Designing Workplace ESOL Courses for Chinese Health-Care Workers at a Boston Nursing Home." In *Teachers as Course Developers*, edited by Kathleen Graves, 39–62. Cambridge: Cambridge University Press, 2001.

CHAPTER 3

Setting Goals for Mentoring

WHAT DO YOU THINK?

1. How important is autonomous learning for teachers learning their profession?
2. What happens when a mentor and mentee hold different views about Question 1? How do they find balance?
3. When you think about benchmarks, do they seem either too broad or too narrow? How could you use them to plan mentoring encounters?
4. How might planning mentoring encounters be similar to or different from planning a unit or course?

Many of us who have worked cross-culturally can remember feeling like a child in the early days of learning to survive in our new society. Perhaps a student grabbed our hand to help us across a busy street. Or a school administrator, seeing our less than proficient chopstick skills, reached across to put food in our bowl. Although it felt awkward, we may have needed some hand-holding or spoon-feeding in those early days. Eventually, though hopefully still with cultural awareness, we were ready to go it alone.

Go it alone is exactly where your mentees eventually need to be. In the introduction, you read about the ultimate goal of mentoring—reflection, self-evaluation, and autonomous learning of teaching. Chapter 2 talked about using benchmarks to identify needs. This chapter talks about how to bridge the gap between needs/benchmarks and classroom instruction—your mentoring encounters, all leading toward the ultimate goal so that you and your mentees know exactly where you're headed in your relationship.

THE ULTIMATE GOAL OF MENTORING

Because we describe the goal as ultimate, let's start with the end of the mentoring process. In many ways, the mentor-mentee relationship is like the teacher-student relationship. In both cases, the experienced person wants the other to know why to do certain things as well as how to do them on their own. In fact, Harmer[1] describes "the ultimate goal of language teaching" as students being able to develop proficiency on their own without the help of a teacher. In the same way, the ultimate goal of the mentoring process is autonomous learning. According to Dom, one of our mentors in training, a mentor's role is to "make things better for [mentees] not by giving them something or doing something for them but by enabling them to make changes and do new things for themselves."[2]

In discussing language learner autonomy, Harmer[3] talks about *empowerment* and Brown and Lee[4] about *strategic investment*. For teachers learning their profession, we like the term *learner ownership* to describe this ultimate goal. The idea appeals to us because it not only incorporates autonomous learning but also evokes a sense of responsibility. You give your mentees voice and engage them in the process of learning teaching. You seek their input about where the relationship is headed and give them choices about how you're going to get there. If necessary, you also give them increasingly greater amounts of control until they take personal responsibility for or rather ownership of the process.

The idea of ownership also seems to fit well with teachers who, as educators, have a better understanding of teaching and learning processes than the average student. However, you shouldn't assume that autonomous learning will come naturally to your mentees. A bent toward spoon-feeding may be rooted in educational traditions or cultural beliefs. For example, in some societies, a certain amount of hand-holding may be expected going down the hierarchy in unequal relationships such as from teacher to student. Or the reasons may be more personal.

IN THEIR OWN WORDS: IS IT CULTURAL OR PERSONAL?

While reflecting on the ultimate goal of mentoring, Sally, a North American, reflects on her experiences with a local teacher in Vietnam and compares them to those of her North American colleagues mentoring teachers in China.

When I interact with my friend, I find her to be a person who is not analytical, evaluative, or introspective. If I were to agree with the [ultimate goal], I would find myself working to change her personality! No, I'm not going to go there. At first, I *was frustrated that we really couldn't talk teaching together. She would complain about her lack of skills, but we couldn't get a conversation going about a lesson or a technique that she'd tried. However, I've come to see that she's just a really, concrete person who takes things at face value (from her perspective) and moves on. It's a bit interesting in light of your comments about Chinese teachers that you've worked with really being focused on improvement. I think that my friend's goals are much simpler. A job with salary and not too much hassle. I think that many teachers (or professionals in many other areas as well) are not really into improvement but job security and stability. I love talking about teaching, but I know that other teachers, in Vietnam, in the US, are not that keyed into improvement, but want to (not completely negatively) get by. Those teachers are hard to mentor! In my interactions with my friend, I am feeling that it's not so much our different cultural backgrounds that confuse the issues sometimes, but rather our very different personalities.*

WHAT DO YOU THINK?

1. How do this mentor's experiences expand on buy-in?
2. If you were writing a reflection on autonomous learning (for teachers learning their profession), how similar or different would it be to the thoughts of this mentor?
3. What are some reasons why your (potential) mentees might be resistant or struggle to take ownership of their learning?
4. How do you feel about learner ownership as a teacher or mentor?

Whether because of cultural or personal reasons, you may find that particular mentees don't readily take ownership of learning teaching. They lack buy-in not only to mentoring but also to taking responsibility for professional development. The answer is not to give up. Instead, be aware that the process may involve a much slower and more arduous slide toward ownership than you expect. It may also require more spoon-feeding and hand-holding at the outset than you're comfortable with. You may need to "shoulder a teacher's burdens part of the way just as a herder carries an exhausted lamb" or at least "go beside" for a time, "nudging" them along toward where they need to be.[5]

Also, be aware of your own potential resistance to learner ownership. One study of how teachers viewed autonomous learning (in self-access centers) concluded that many felt professionally isolated in such contexts because they needed to have constant feedback from the students in regular classes to give themselves a sense of their teaching progress.[6] What is your reaction to this as a mentor? Do you need to see your mentees' progress in order to feel you are doing a good job? Do you feel like you're being irresponsible if you don't exercise some control over the process?

The ultimate goal affects every aspect of the mentoring relationship and comes into play at all stages of the process. In Chapter 2, we talked about how identifying needs in negotiation with your mentees gives them voice and personal investment. In the next few paragraphs, you'll see how drawing them into articulating goals also gives them a sense of ownership that will carry them through to the end.

FROM BENCHMARKS TO MENTORING ENCOUNTERS

When planning the specifics of where you and your mentees are headed, keeping the big picture, the ultimate goal, in view is vital. It's also important to keep benchmarks in mind. Benchmarks, as we noted in Chapter 2, are a good way of identifying needs. They provide an efficient way of determining starting and continuing points.

What benchmarks don't do is bridge the gap between needs and classroom instruction, which for you is specific mentoring encounters. Focusing on the ultimate goal keeps the end result in mind. Benchmarks keep the smaller goals or steps along the way in view. Yet, benchmarks are broad, and you may still have a difficult time envisioning the even smaller steps taken in a unit of mentoring (a series of mentoring encounters). One way to depict these steps is to write outcomes. Another way is the use of essential questions.

Outcomes

Because you are a language teacher, we won't insult you with the specific details of writing outcomes. You've likely developed your own version of the well-used SWBAT-pattern (*Students should/will be able to . . .*) and design aims that are SMART (Specific, Measurable, Attainable, Reasonable, and Time-limited).[7] What you may not have thought about is writing outcomes for mentoring encounters.

Outcomes can be written for one mentoring encounter or a series of encounters. They can be SMART and follow a SWBAT-pattern or a pattern you have developed for your own teaching that you're more comfortable with. Like benchmarks, they can encompass *knowledge* and *skills* aims as well as *affect* and *values*.

Although written for a more traditional course, the aims presented in "Here's What Happened: A Teaching Methodology Course in China" may give you a better picture of what mentoring outcomes can look like.

HERE'S WHAT HAPPENED: A TEACHING METHODOLOGY COURSE IN CHINA

Melody has been teaching a teaching methodology course for a number of years to MA students in China. In each session, she aims toward outcomes that take students (her mentees) through all levels of Bloom's Taxonomy and also an additional *values* level. Recently she learned how to frame goals as essential questions. Below you can see her original outcomes for a unit on teaching writing, followed by their reframing as essential questions.

Unit Outcomes

By the end of this unit, you should be able to:
1. Explain background information and important issues related to teaching writing.
2. List and describe some writing skills and strategies.
3. Describe how to set up a writing lesson and why each part is important.
4. Analyze and evaluate the way you teach writing or the way it is taught in your country.
5. Create a writing lesson.
6. Make moral decisions about what it means to be a responsible writing teacher.

Essential Questions

1. What does a writing lesson look like?
2. What does a principled blueprint for writing instruction include?
3. How have you constructed writing instruction?
4. How can we teach writing rightly?

WHAT DO YOU THINK?

1. What benefits do you see to articulating outcomes for your mentoring encounters?
2. In "Here's What Happened: A Teaching Methodology Course in China," you see both outcomes and essential questions. Which do you like better as a means of planning for and guiding mentoring encounters? Why?
3. What benefits might essential questions have?

Essential Questions

As Melody's experiences suggest, another way of building a bridge from benchmarks to mentoring encounters is essential questions. They are outcomes framed as questions intended to organize learning around inquiry that leads toward end results and beyond. While they haven't necessarily caught on in many English language teaching settings, they have been used in other situations to (1) help teachers focus learning on what is most important,[8] (2) make connections between standards, students, and the world, and then connect this learning to assessments,[9] and (3) engage hard to motivate students through inquiry.[10] Like Melody's course, they've also been used to reorganize a secondary English methods course such that students explored "pervasive myths regarding the education of emergent bilingual learners."[11] Below are examples of questions from one session early in the course, aiming toward a benchmark that could be expressed: *understanding bilingual learner identity*.

1. "Who are English Learners (ELs)?"
2. "What experiences do they bring to the classroom?"[12]

In many ways, essential questions are well suited to the process of learning teaching. They are described as "open-ended" and "thought-provoking," requiring "higher-order thinking" and "support and justification"; they raise "additional questions" while leading toward "transferable ideas within (and sometimes across) disciplines."[13] As you head toward reflection and self-evaluation with your mentees, the questions that come up in your mentoring encounters fit this description. They inspire discussion and deeper thought. One question often has multiple possible answers, each supported in various ways given different settings and circumstances. However, an answer in one setting is quite possibly transferable to another although it's just as likely to raise more questions.

IN THEIR OWN WORDS: REFRAMING OUTCOMES AS ESSENTIAL QUESTIONS

Melody reflects on the process of reframing outcomes as essential questions and how it affected her teaching and student learning.

When I first started using essential questions in Teaching Methodology, it changed my way of thinking about teaching. In the early days of teaching this course, I knew that my students were used to a more traditional approach to learning, so I aimed for the middle ground between what they were comfortable with and my more learner-centered, discovery learning approach. The longer I taught, though, the more I realized that what I was doing wasn't having much *effect. They were leaving my course still intending to teach English in the way they had been taught. I would have been satisfied with this if I thought they were making decisions out of reflection and autonomous thought rather than falling back on the familiar. And so I leaned further and further toward my end, hoping the experience would inspire new ways of thinking.*

What essential questions did was take the responsibility for thinking and learning off my shoulders and place it on my students' shoulders. By designing each unit around 3–4 essential questions, I stopped looking for what I could give them so that I could draw them up to a pinnacle I had planned for them. Instead, as they pursued the answers to questions through activities I planned, they did the work, even to a certain extent deciding on the pinnacle and how to get there. On course feedback, the students described the process this way:

> **Student 1:** *In the past, I think teaching is only the teacher's duty, that it is only teachers who make great effort so that students can get a lot. However, I realized that teaching and learning connect with each other. Only if both teacher and students engage in class will there be a good teaching result.*
> **Student 2:** *I used to teach knowledge directly to students. But now I think students can learn by themselves. And students can have an impression on what they discovered.*
> **Student 3:** *Maybe we were more focused on put in before we learned this lesson. But now I focus more on the balance between put in and put out.*

One reason for using essential questions is to support learner ownership. Instead of stating outcomes, you present aims as questions to be explored through a mentoring encounter. The point is not for you to frame and then answer the questions. Rather, you pique your mentees' curiosity by approaching the encounter as a puzzle to be solved. Then, you engage them in finding answers. Although in a classroom essential questions are usually framed by teachers, they can at times be negotiated with students. Even more so should they be negotiated with and framed by your mentees as you move toward autonomous learning. In "Here's What Happened: A Teaching Methodology Course in China," which piques your curiosity and draws you into the process of learning: Melody's outcomes or her essential questions?

Another reason for using essential questions is that they may come across to your mentees as softer than traditional outcomes. The last chapter acknowledged your potential concerns about coming across as pejorative to your mentees. Negotiating outcomes is one way to lessen any sort of face threat. Wording outcomes as essential questions may take that softening one step further. As a language teacher, you've likely taught your students this aspect of sociocultural competence, that one way to mitigate is to ask a question rather than make a statement.[14] In "Here's What Happened: A Teaching Methodology Course in China," which seems softer to you: Melody's outcomes or her essential questions?

Affect and *values* outcomes, in particular, may be softened when framed as essential questions. When talking about heart and soul issues, you may feel like a busybody interfering in the lives of your mentees. Offering them the autonomy to identify and then word outcomes as questions mitigates potentially sensitive topics and gives them ownership of any needed change. Moreover, because your values come into play too, the exercise of negotiating essential questions may make it easier for both of you to let go, listen, and learn from each other. In "Here's What Happened: A Teaching Methodology Course in China," which do you feel more willing to explore with a mentee: Melody's outcomes or her essential questions?

SETTING UP A MENTORING PLAN

Tracy, one of our mentors in training, reflected on a semester of mentoring through an online discussion forum and decided that it was not as organized as she would have liked. She was also looking for ways to increase participation. Her solution was to design a syllabus for her mentoring encounters. The syllabus, she explained, was as much for her benefit—to keep her mentoring structured and consistent, as it was for the benefit of her mentees—to give them an overview of where they were headed and encourage participation.

Tracy's idea made an impression and led us to view the mentoring process much like teaching a course. That's why in this chapter and the last we've been talking about assessing needs, identifying benchmarks, articulating outcomes or essential questions, and designing a syllabus, or, in other words, setting up a mentoring plan. You'll have an opportunity to work your way through some of these steps and design your own mentoring plan in "Now It's Your Turn."

At the end of the chapter, you will also find two examples of mentoring plans. The first is Tracy's. After reflecting on her need for structure, she designed this plan for a new semester of mentoring. She's no longer running an online forum but working one-on-one with one teacher and setting up an action research project with a different group of teachers (in part to complete assignments for our course). The second plan is Sarah and Steve's. After their "Puzzle It Out: Distance Mentoring in the Middle East" in Chapter 2, you may have been wondering what they decided to do. We like the steps they took in order to meet the needs of their mentees. We also like the fact that both they and Tracy started with our template and then took ownership of it in order to make it theirs. In fact, we revised our template after seeing their plans.

One of the challenges that Tracy, Sarah, and Steve have faced is mentee buy-in. Negotiating a mentoring plan with mentees and giving them ownership of the process is one way to increase their investment as is designing your plan as part of a mentoring contract. What also helps is the structure that a plan offers. Tracy, Sarah, and Steve made expectations clear about how and when mentoring would occur and the roles mentor and mentee would play.

Because our mentors were completing assignments for our course, they laid out their plans before talking to their mentees (though they already had a good understanding of needs and which benchmarks to aim toward). At this point for whatever reason, you may be working through the steps in "Now It's Your Turn" on your own. However, as our mentors did (We hope!), before implementing your plan, you'll need to go back and negotiate the details with your mentees and so encourage them to take ownership of the process.

NOW IT'S YOUR TURN

Task 3.1: Outcomes or Essential Questions

Which do you prefer, outcomes or essential questions? Which might work better with your current or future mentees?

1. Choose a few benchmarks you could work toward with a (potential) mentee. Brainstorm for outcomes and then essential questions that express some of the smaller steps that might lead to reaching the benchmark (the aims for a mentoring encounter). We've used Melody's outcomes and essential questions as an example in Table 3.1.

Table 3.1 **Outcomes or Essential Questions**

Benchmark	Outcomes	Essential Questions
Understand principles of English language teaching.	By the end of this unit, you should be able to explain background information related to teaching writing.	What does a principled blueprint for writing instruction include?

2. Discuss your preferences (outcomes or essential questions) in your mentoring journal or with your mentor support group. Also talk about which might work better with your current or future mentees.
3. If you are currently mentoring, repeat this task with your mentee(s) and decide together whether you will use outcomes or essential questions.

Task 3.2: Mentoring Plan

Drawing on what you learned from your needs analysis in Task 2.4 (Chapter 2), plan for a series of mentoring encounters. Or using what you discussed with your mentor support group in Task 2.3, project what this plan might look like for your potential mentees. Use the Mentoring Plan Template in Table 3.2 at the end of the chapter, but feel free to adapt it as our mentors in training have done. (See their examples at the end of the chapter in Tables 3.3 and 3.4.) You should view this plan as an outline. Later in the book, particularly in Section IV: Task-Based Mentoring, you'll have an opportunity to revise and plan the details of specific mentoring encounters.

Task 3.3: Mentoring Contract

You started this contract in Task 1.2 (Chapter 1). Now, with the completion of your Mentoring Plan, you're ready to finish it.

Task 3.4: Taking Ownership

If you are currently mentoring, who is taking ownership of learning, you or your mentee?

1. Below is a list of decisions you've been asked to make with your mentee so far. (Task numbers are in parentheses.) Who has taken responsibility for each decision? Put the decisions on a scale like the mentor-mentee scale in Figure 3.1 below. If you have shared responsibility, some of them may go in the middle.
    - Defining mentor (1.1)
    - Deciding when, where, and how you will meet (1.2)
    - Determining what the relationship looks like and why you're engaging in it (1.3)
    - Choosing terms (*benchmarks, standards,* or another term) (2.2)
    - Articulating benchmarks/standards for teachers (2.3)
    - Identifying which benchmarks to work toward (2.3, 2.4)
    - Choosing between outcomes and essential questions (3.1)

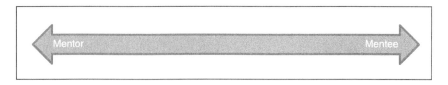

Figure 3.1 Learner Ownership Scale

- Identifying and articulating outcomes or essential questions (3.2)
- Deciding what modules will appear in your mentoring plan (3.2)
- Determining which approaches you will take in your mentoring encounters (3.2)

2. Once you've completed the scale, answer the questions below. (Remember that your starting point may be somewhere in the middle. You may need, for example, to take more ownership until your mentee grows beyond survival skills in the classroom.)
   - Are you and your mentee in a good place?
   - If not, what steps could you take in order to encourage more ownership?

Table 3.2 **Mentoring Plan Template**

BENCHMARKS: *What's the next step for the mentee? Which benchmark(s) should you work toward?*
COURSE OUTCOMES OR ESSENTIAL QUESTIONS: *In this coming period of mentoring, which outcomes will you be working toward, or what essential questions will you be answering?*
OUTLINE: *In order to reach outcomes or answer essential questions, what steps will you take? What time frame will you be working in (schedule)? What will your mentoring encounters focus on (modules)? What tasks, methods, or forums will work best to reach outcomes or answer essential questions (approach)?*

Schedule:	Modules:	Approach:

Table 3.3 **Tracy's Mentoring Plan**

Professional Development Opportunities for Spring 2017	
Video Observation and Reflection:	
Purpose:	For the teacher to use self as an observer and to practice reflective teaching.
Method:	The teacher will video targeted segments of classes throughout the semester and answer specific feedback questions on what they observed. Video segments should be 4–10 minutes, and will be shared with the mentor to inform discussions. Insights will be shared with the mentor biweekly (Weeks 2, 4, and 6).
Time commitment:	Approximately 1 hour a week for 6 weeks.
Start Date:	March 13th **End Date:** May 1st
Plan:	Week 1—Video #1—Openings Week 2—Video #2—Closings Week 3—Video #3—Choose 1 from the following: vocabulary activity, instructions for multi-stage activities, communicative activities. Week 4—Video #4—Choose from the following: pacing, textbooks in the classroom, using technology in the classroom. Week 5—Video #5—Feedback to students/error correction, classroom management, student participation strategies. Week 6—Video #6—Choose one of the above not yet attempted.
Development through Classroom Research	
Purpose:	For the teacher to learn more about the teaching context and to practice common research methods.
Method:	The teachers will work as a team with the mentor and a local teacher to assemble a literature review, design and publish a survey, and report findings on a research question.
Time commitment:	Approximately 1 hour a week for 8–9 weeks.
Start Date:	March 6th **End Date:** May 1st
Plan:	Week 1—Develop survey questions (and get them translated) Week 2—Publish (disseminate) survey Week 3—Gather data (academic articles related to research question) Week 4—Gather data and begin documenting survey responses Week 5—Gather data and begin analysis/synthesis of research Week 6—Complete analysis of survey data and consider further data needs Week 7—Compile data and brainstorm application to current teaching plan Week 8—Discussion of whether findings could be published

Table 3.4 **Sarah and Steve's Mentoring Plan**

Faculty Meetings—Semester Focus: Needs Analysis for a Scope and Sequence, Spring 2017

	Content	Pre-Work	Description of Meeting	Product
1	**Creating Scope and Sequence**	Bring textbooks, materials and the schedule for one class for the spring semester with you to your faculty meeting.	In your first faculty meeting you will fill in a scope and sequence form we will provide, for one of your courses, using your textbooks/materials.	*First draft of one scope and sequence—Emailed to your mentors and faculty coordinator.
2	**Needs Analysis: Past**	Conduct an interview of a teacher or student(s) before coming to your faculty meeting about their past learning experiences based on a form we will email you. You must complete this before your meeting. (Another option could be an observation of a class at one level before yours. For example, if you are teaching university, you would observe high school).	In this meeting, you will learn more about the educational backgrounds of your students so that you can better understand their present learning preferences and language learning experiences. Discuss your findings as a group. Fill in a learner profile form that will be provided for you.	*A compiled learner profile (past) that outlines the typical background of the students within your school's context. It could have separate headings if your group has separate contexts. (one form per group compiled/completed during the meeting). The profile can have separate sections for children and adults—Emailed to your mentors by the faculty coordinator.
3	**Needs Analysis: Present**	Before this meeting we will send examples of needs analysis surveys that you can choose or adapt from. Survey your students or administration about current learning preferences, motivations, and overall perceived needs. Try to target the same course that you created the scope and sequence for.	In this meeting, report to your group the results of your surveys and discuss the present needs of your students. Fill in a learner profile form that will be provided for you.	*Create a group learner profile (present) based on the data from the surveys. The profile can have separate sections for children and adults—Emailed to your mentors by the faculty coordinator.

Faculty Meetings—Semester Focus: Needs Analysis for a Scope and Sequence, Spring 2017

	Content	Pre-Work	Description of Meeting	Product
4	Needs Analysis: Future	Contact a student(s) who is a step ahead of your current students. For example, if you teach university, find someone who came from your university and is now in the workforce. If you teach refugees, try to contact a friend of a student that is already settled in the West. Complete an email survey or interview. If you teach children you could do an observation or email a colleague.	Report the findings of your email interview (or observation) to your group. Discuss the differences between students' perceived needs (present) and actual needs (future). Reflect as a group on how this might influence your teaching.	*Create a group learner profile (future) based on the data from the surveys based on a form provided to you. The profile can have separate sections for children and adults—Emailed to your mentors by the faculty coordinator.
5	Revising Scope and Sequence	Reflect on your scope and sequence based on the data you collected that was compiled in the three learner profiles. Make changes to your scope and sequence and bring both the old and new with you to the meeting.	Discuss the changes you made to your scope and sequence and have a time of peer feedback on the changes you made.	Email the revised scope and sequence to your mentors and faculty coordinator.

NOTES

1. Jeremy Harmer, *The Practice of English Language Teaching*, 5th ed. (Harlow: Pearson Education, 2015), 97.
2. Melissa K. Smith and Marilyn Lewis, "Toward Facilitative Mentoring and Catalytic Interventions," *ELT Journal* 69, no. 2 (2015): 143, https:/doi.org/10.1093/elt/ccu075.
3. Harmer, *The Practice of English Language Teaching*.
4. H. Douglas Brown and Heekyeong Lee, *Teaching by Principles*, 4th ed. (White Plains, NY: Pearson Education, 2015).
5. Smith and Lewis, *ELT Journal*, 9.

6. Hayo Reinders and Noemi Lazaro, "Beliefs, Identity and Motivation in Implementing Autonomy: The Teacher's Perspective," in *Identity, Motivation and Autonomy in Language Learning*, ed. Garold Murray, Xuesong Gao, and Terry Lamb (Bristol: Multilingual Matters, 2011): 125–142.
7. See, for example, Harmer, *The Practice of English Language Teaching*, 216–217.
8. Jonathan Ostenson and Elizabeth Gleason-Sutton, "Making the Classics Matter to Students through Digital Literacies and Essential Questions," *The English Journal* 101, no. 2 (2011), www.jstor.org/stable/41415423.
9. Julie Gorlewski, "Research for the Classroom: Standards, Standardization, and Student Learning," *The English Journal* 102, no. 5 (2013), www.jstor.org/stable/24484101.
10. Douglas Fisher and Nancy Frey, "Motivating Boys to Read: Inquiry, Modeling, and Choice Matter," *Journal of Adolescent and Adult Literacy* 55, no. 7 (2012): 587–596, https:/doi.org/10.1002/JAAL.00070.
11. Mileidis Gort and Wendy J. Glenn, "Navigating Tensions in the Process of Change: An English Educator's Dilemma Management in the Revision and Implementation of a Diversity-Infused Methods Course," *Research in the Teaching of English* 45, no. 1 (2010): 64, https:/doi.org/10.2307/25704896.
12. Ibid., 69.
13. Jay McTighe and Grant Wiggins, *Essential Questions: Opening Doors to Student Understanding* (Alexandria, VA: ASCD, 2013), Kindle edition, chap. 1.
14. Tasha Bleistein, Melissa K. Smith, and Marilyn Lewis, *Teaching Speaking* (Alexandria, VA: TESOL International Association, 2013).

REFERENCES

Bleistein, Tasha, Melissa K. Smith, and Marilyn Lewis. *Teaching Speaking*. Alexandria, VA: TESOL International Association, 2013.

Brown, H. Douglas and Heekyeong Lee. *Teaching by Principles*. 4th ed. White Plains, NY: Pearson Education, 2015.

Fisher, Douglas and Nancy Frey. "Motivating Boys to Read: Inquiry, Modeling, and Choice Matter." *Journal of Adolescent and Adult Literacy* 55, no. 7 (2012): 587–596. https:/doi.org/10.1002/JAAL.00070.

Gorlewski, Julie. "Research for the Classroom: Standards, Standardization, and Student Learning." *The English Journal* 102, no. 5 (2013): 84–88. www.jstor.org/stable/24484101.

Gort, Mileidis and Wendy J. Glenn. "Navigating Tensions in the Process of Change: An English Educator's Dilemma Management in the Revision and Implementation of a Diversity-Infused Methods Course." *Research in the Teaching of English* 45, no. 1 (2010): 59–86. https:/doi.org/10.2307/25704896.

Harmer, Jeremy. *The Practice of English Language Teaching*. 5th ed. Harlow: Pearson Education, 2015.

McTighe, Jay and Grant Wiggins. *Essential Questions: Opening Doors to Student Understanding*. Alexandria, VA: ASCD, 2013. Kindle edition.

Ostenson, Jonathan and Elizabeth Gleason-Sutton. "Making the Classics Matter to Students through Digital Literacies and Essential Questions." *The English Journal* 101, no. 2 (2011): 37–43. www.jstor.org/stable/41415423.

Reinders, Hayo and Noemi Lazaro. "Beliefs, Identity and Motivation in Implementing Autonomy: The Teacher's Perspective." In *Identity, Motivation and Autonomy in Language Learning*, edited by Garold Murray, Xuesong Gao, and Terry Lamb, 125–142. Bristol: Multilingual Matters, 2011.

Smith, Melissa K. and Marilyn Lewis. "Toward Facilitative Mentoring and Catalytic Interventions." *ELT Journal* 69, no. 2 (2015): 140–150. https:/doi.org/10.1093/elt/ccu075.

SECTION II

Mentoring in Context

At one point in my career I was sent to train teachers of English in a country that was in the middle of a civil war. Amongst my roles was the mentoring of people who had already been teachers of one foreign language but who were now required to teach a different language, namely English, at the secondary school level. As time went by I became aware of a number of interwoven cultural factors.

—Nessie

It has struck me again and perhaps more acutely—that I am really being pulled in three different directions. There is the way my faith tells me to live, act, teach, and mentor; there is the way my culture tells me to do these things; and there is the way my host culture tells me to do these things. I'm beginning to think that it is really a rare instance when all three of these directions really intersect. Yet I live in this tension.

—Karen

CHAPTER 4

The Classroom Context

WHAT DO YOU THINK?

1. What factors make it easy or difficult for two people to cooperate as mentor and mentee?
2. What personal or cultural boundaries might you have to cross in your current or future mentoring?
3. What personal or cultural boundaries do your (potential) mentees have to cross in their classrooms?
4. What aspects of the classroom context do mentors need to understand in order to help mentees?
5. How can you learn about your (potential) mentees' classroom contexts?

Communication problems can come in many varieties. Sometimes we get lost in a conversation because we haven't been listening and miss the context. For the sake of our relationship, we probably ought to admit our inattentiveness rather than pretending. In our second language, the problem can be exacerbated by a lack of proficiency. When we've lost the thread, we may never find it without some extra humility and help.

As you'll see later in this book, mentoring encounters most often take the form of conversations. Whether formal or informal, face-to-face, or virtual, in same or cross-cultural settings, mentors can get lost in them if they're not following the thread. In other words, if you don't understand the settings within which your mentees teach, how can you help them down the path toward proficiency in the classroom? The context influences the direction of your mentoring encounters. Moreover, demonstrating a willingness to understand may deepen your mentoring relationships. Rather than feigning an understanding of the context, you're better off taking on a learner role before attempting to offer help.

CONTEXTS OF TEACHING AND MENTORING

According to Freeman and Johnson,[1] one of the domains that make up the knowledge base for teachers is social context. It refers to the cultural norms and social institutions that shape teaching and learning, both currently and across history. When Brown and Lee[2] discuss contexts of learning and teaching, they look broadly at factors like culture and policy and also more narrowly at learner factors like age and proficiency levels. Harmer[3] talks about a "learning culture" and how teachers need to analyze the contexts within which they teach, including looking at how culture, popular culture, and personal factors influence views of learning and teaching. In her chapter on the context of English language teaching, Schellekens[4] mentions diversity as "one of the main defining characteristics." She illustrates the word with mention of the different languages spoken by students, their varied reasons for being in class, and the different skills they bring (such as plus or minus literacy).

How do all these differing factors work together to make up your mentees' teaching contexts? An MA TESOL (Teaching English to Speakers of Other Languages) course we have taught is entitled Classroom Dynamics Practicum in TESOL. The *Collins English Dictionary*[5] defines *dynamics* as "the various forces, physical, oral, economic, etc., operating in any field," and "the way such forces shift or change in relation to one another." *Dynamics* seems to be a good descriptor for the different contexts within which your mentees work.

Figure 4.1 illustrates the dynamics at work in a classroom. At the heart of a classroom are the human forces. Chapter 2 noted that students are what drive classroom decisions. However, students are not the only human force operating in a classroom. They function in relation to the teacher. Central to these human forces, each individual's personal characteristics, beliefs, and experiences interact to shape what happens in the classroom. Shaping also comes from outside forces like institutional expectations, values inherent in schools and education systems, and cultural and societal norms. All these inside and outside forces shape classroom dynamics, including the relationships between learners and teachers and their roles and responsibilities.

Your mentoring context is largely made up of your mentees' teaching contexts. However, in your interactions with them, the same factors that influence their classrooms also affect your mentoring. Inside and outside

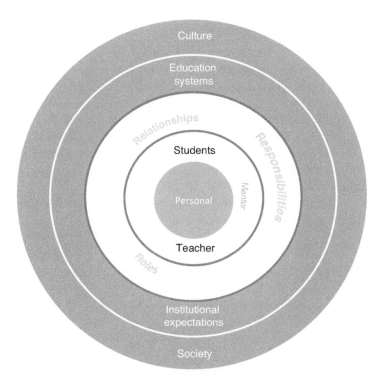

Figure 4.1 Contexts of Teaching and Mentoring

forces shape dynamics, including the relationship between you and your mentees and your roles and responsibilities.

This chapter and the next aim to make these abstract categories come alive for you, the mentor, as you intrude on this picture (as unobtrusively as possible). This chapter discusses the classroom context and zooms in on the personal forces at work as teachers and learners relate and fulfill their responsibilities, keeping the outside forces in view as they shape classroom dynamics. The next chapter will go into more detail about the broader context, the outside forces that form the backdrop behind your mentees' classroom contexts.

CLASSROOM DYNAMICS FOR MENTORS

Talking about every possible aspect of your mentees' classroom contexts would be impossible. Instead, we'll start with some examples, and then we'll move on to suggestions for how you can become versed in their classrooms so that contextualized mentoring is possible.

Tensions in the Classroom Context

In any classroom, the context is made up of forces that may extend from one extreme to another. Personal factors can cause these tensions. Obviously, they are influenced and sometimes exacerbated by outside forces, especially when crossing cultures. In the following paragraphs, some of the human dynamics at work in a classroom are described as a series of potential tensions. They bring up points touched on earlier in this book. They are not only ones your mentees may face in their classroom context, but also ones you may face in your mentoring relationships.

The example tensions below are first illustrated by Chinese proverbs. In recent years, the West has developed a fascination with the Chinese education system. In popular culture, news headlines like the following are not unusual: "Half of Primary Schools Set to Teach Maths Chinese-style."[6] This interest in Chinese education (and our own experiences with it as teachers and mentors) inspired us to frame our example tensions under Chinese proverbs that we had discussed in a support group with Chinese teachers. Some of their ideas and reflections are included below. The tensions are further illustrated by "Here's what happened: Co-Teaching and Co-Mentoring." Each tension is reviewed from your perspective as a mentor, and then you're given an opportunity to decide how much it plays a role in your mentees' classroom contexts.

HERE'S WHAT HAPPENED: CO-TEACHING AND CO-MENTORING

As coordinator of an intensive English program at a university in the United States, Asa was asked if he would supervise a practicum student working on an undergraduate degree in TESOL at a nearby college. Because of previous experiences, he approached the task from a mentoring rather than a supervisory perspective. He also approached it as a relationship. In fact, he couldn't imagine mentoring someone with whom he did not have a relationship. Although not all of his previous mentees were easy for him to relate to, building a relationship with his new one was natural. From the start, they hit it off. They had similar personalities and shared a sense of humor. He had a degree from her college, an institution that had shaped their shared worldview and their motivation to approach teaching as an act of service. First, she shadowed him, and they co-planned. Then she led activities and eventually taught lessons in his classes. Although he fulfilled certain supervisory responsibilities (observing, giving feedback, and filling out paperwork), he started to feel like they were co-teaching. They experienced the classroom together, sharing victories, figuring out challenges, and bearing defeats. Asa did not view himself as her supervisor. Rather he saw them as co-planners, co-teachers, and perhaps even co-mentors.

WHAT DO YOU THINK?

1. Although for Asa this mentoring experience was overwhelmingly positive, what tensions might he have faced?
2. What tensions might he have faced in previous experiences?
3. What tensions have you faced in your mentoring or do you picture facing if you are about to start?
4. How are those tensions similar to ones your (potential) mentees might face in their classrooms?

授人以鱼不如授人以渔 *Giving Someone a Fish Is Not as Good as Teaching a Person How to Fish*

The English version of this proverb reads, "Give a man fish and feed him for a day; teach a man to fish and feed him for a lifetime." The Chinese teachers in our support group feel this tension. They know autonomy is good for learners and in our discussion listed specific ways they cultivate ownership in their students. Yet, both the exam system and tradition drive them toward spoon-feeding or more accurately 填鸭式教育 ("stuffing the duck education"), which likens teaching to a marketplace practice of feeding a duck until food literally spews from its mouth. (The duck then weighs more and garners a higher price.)

As you've reflected on ideas in this book so far, perhaps you've already sensed a tension between the mentoring relationship and autonomous learning. Inherent in a relationship like the one Asa was trying to build is a sense of banding together, co-learning, co-teaching, and co-development, which may seem like hand-holding. On the other side stands the goal of learner ownership. Personal differences, sometimes influenced by outside forces such as education systems and traditions, can also trigger tensions within your mentees, between them and you, and them and their students.

WHAT DO YOU THINK?

1. Do your (potential) mentees face tensions like this in their classroom contexts?
2. How do they view autonomous learning and learner ownership? What tensions, if any, exist between their views and those of their students?
3. What kinds of relationships are your mentees attempting to build with their students? What tension, if any, exists between their expectations of the teacher-student relationship and those of their students?
4. How do their ideas differ from yours?
5. How might these tensions in your mentees' classroom contexts affect your mentoring relationship?

教书育人 *Teach Books; Educate Human Beings*

When asked to analyze this proverb, the Chinese teachers taking part in our support group spoke of both the academic and moral development of their students. Their English textbooks often include topics and readings that teach values like diligence, honesty, or respect for people. Moreover, the teachers feel a burden to be both an academic and moral model for their students and sense a responsibility to look after their well-being in every realm. One university English teacher recounted an incident in which a student slashed her bicycle tires. When they happened to meet later and he seemed embarrassed, she reassured him he had her forgiveness. Although he never finished his degree, she expressed relief that he'd admitted his "folly," had found employment, and seemed to be taking his place in society. She humbly refused to admit the role her kindness played in his growth.

When we first introduced the topic of *affect* and *values* needs, we acknowledged the personal dilemma you may face in bringing them into a mentoring relationship. However, the tension goes beyond the personal. Outside factors come into play as well. In some cultures (like China) and some settings (like Asa's where there was a shared worldview with his mentee and her undergraduate institution), mentors may be expected to delve into the moral dimension. In other settings, doing so might seem out of place or unwelcome. In describing the history of moral education in the American public education system, for example, Brimi[7] acknowledges the current setting as "an era when we are careful not to impose unwanted beliefs on others," pressure that seems to come from both within and without. He suggests that given the diversity in classroom contexts, teachers "may be wise in choosing not to address moral issues."[8] Does this also mean that in similar settings, mentors should not explore *values* benchmarks with their mentees?

WHAT DO YOU THINK?

1. Do your (potential) mentees face tensions like this in their classroom contexts?
2. How do they view the *affect* and *values* needs of their students?
3. Do they feel responsible for meeting them? Or do they believe that is not their role? Why?
4. How are their ideas different from yours?
5. How might these tensions in your mentees' classroom contexts affect your mentoring?

一日为师终身为父 One Day a Teacher, Forever a Father

The support group participants see two sides to this proverb: (1) students' respect for teachers, and (2) teachers' care for students. When asked to illustrate, one teacher, Ma Ping, told about a student who missed the first two weeks of their college English course. The third week, he finally appeared but without his textbook and unable (or unwilling) to answer any of her questions. At first, Ma Ping was affronted by his apparent disrespect. She recounts what happened next:

> After class, I reflected on his behavior. I decided to go his dormitory. The following day at 12 o'clock I knocked at his door with some chicken legs. He opened the door with a surprised but tired facial expression. I was surprised to see that the room was nearly dark because the curtains had not been drawn, but there was something shining on the table. Oh, that was a computer, and he was playing a computer game. I helped him to draw the curtains and held up the chicken legs in front of his nose. He was shocked, but I also found some tears in his eyes. Later we talked about his attitude, and he told me that he'd heard students did not have to work hard in our university. They just needed to pass exams, and they could graduate. He also told me he'd heard that our university was poor academically. After hearing his words, I patiently and firmly said, "How do you know about our university if you yourself do not attend class?"

Ma Ping's parenting of this student met with positive results. He became "a top student" and came to class every day "with a shining face." She ended her story by explaining, "He describes me with two adjectives, *devoted* and *affectionate*."

In Chapter 1, you saw suggestions for where to end up on each of the mentoring continuums. Because of their similarities, Asa and his mentee seemed to have little trouble agreeing on balance points. However, personal and cultural factors can complicate the process. In settings like China, teachers (and also mentors) are afforded great respect, and with that comes great responsibility. Traditionally, they have been granted authority and charged with duty in the classroom that may in some ways still resemble the role fathers played in China's ancient patriarchal society. For Westerners like us working in China, finding balance is complicated by the inside and outside forces influencing our mentees.

Authority structures like these can also affect your mentees' views of evaluation and development. Regardless of your efforts to build co-relationships and however development-focused your approach, they may view you as an authority in the role of evaluator. If you're mentoring across such a boundary, your starting point may be much closer to the middle of the continuum than you are comfortable with. Personal differences within both hierarchical and egalitarian societies can also play a role in your starting point.

WHAT DO YOU THINK?

1. Do your (potential) mentees face tensions like this in their classroom contexts?
2. How do they view authority, respect, and responsibility? What tension, if any, exists between their views and their students'?
3. How do they find appropriate balance points on the continuum between their views and those of their students?
4. How might these tensions in your mentees' classroom contexts affect your mentoring?

Researching the Classroom Context

In answering the questions listed under each tension above, you may have discovered a complexity of factors shaping your mentees' classroom dynamics (and your mentoring context). Moreover, the small selection of examples above may only give you a surface understanding of your mentees' classroom settings. How can you deepen your understanding? In *The Art of Crossing Cultures*, Storti[9] suggests that when faced with a cultural incident (a situation in which our assumptions are unmet), we observe and learn so that we can develop culturally appropriate expectations. In your mentoring encounters where you or your mentee are crossing cultures in your relationship, in the classroom, or both, Storti's advice seems wise. In fact, you may want to become a researcher of your mentees' classroom contexts where they are your primary cultural informants as you follow the suggestions below.

Ask Questions

When you see the word *research*, you may feel excited about further understanding your mentees' classroom contexts. Or your affective filter might go up at the associations the word has in your place of work. However, *research* "simply means trying to find answers to questions, an activity every one of us does all the time to learn more about the world around us."[10] Questions, as you'll see later in this book, play a huge role in giving feedback to mentees. Setting the stage for those interactions, they are also an important step toward mentoring in context.

Posing questions about the Chinese proverbs to teachers in our support group first showed us how they fit traditionally and currently into Chinese society. Further inquiry revealed how the teachers' experiences influence their personal understandings of the proverbs. Eventually we saw how they admire the proverbs as an ideal, a goal to aim toward but don't necessarily enact them as a way of life and teaching.

Dig Deeper

In their fascination with Chinese education, popular culture in the West seems to have gained only a surface understanding. Digging deeper, the title of an article suggests that although there are many reasons to admire the Chinese education system, it may be "Flunking Innovation and Creativity."[11] Using the Chinese educators in our support group as informants, we learn that outside large cities like Shanghai (where many comparative tests results have come from), other regions, especially rural areas, are falling behind. Our informants who are also parents reveal that in order to compensate, students in less developed areas (starting in elementary school) may have five or more hours of homework every weekday, sleep no more than six hours each night, and have extra homework or attend extra classes on weekends.

When you're asking questions in order to understand your mentees' classroom contexts, you may need to probe. Personal and cultural factors can be complex. Figuring them out can be complicated by the inside and outside forces at work in you that give birth to your assumptions about what should happen in the classroom. You can also be confused by informants who are trying to be polite or who struggle to make a distinction between reality and the ideal.

Show Genuine Curiosity

To take an example of mentoring from a different field, a medical social worker was explaining how she assesses what her patients understand about their diagnosis, prognosis, and treatment options. Her conversations with them flow naturally out of her need to understand what is not her primary field. In other words, her curiosity is genuine as she seeks to help them. Although language learning and teaching are your primary field, your mentees are the experts in their particular classroom contexts. They are your informants, and you are the eager learner who, like the social worker, not only listens but also enters into their victories and challenges.

Often this happens naturally, but you can also feed your curiosity. That's what happened in our support group. Initially our discussions focused around language, culture, or education topics we were versed in. When we switched to proverbs, the teachers became the experts in language, culture, and education. We were fascinated by what they taught us and also inspired to learn more.

Draw on Relevant Outside Sources

Your mentees are your primary informants about their classroom contexts; however, both you and they will benefit from drawing on relevant outside sources, especially if they are new to the context. Consider, for example, Sarah's situation. A group of her mentees are teaching refugees in the Middle East who are waiting for placement in other countries. Her mentees, new to the region and the education setting, do not yet fully understand their classrooms contexts. They, as much as Sarah, have benefited from reading articles and observing and talking to other teachers with more experience in this area.

Outside sources may also be necessary when the forces influencing classroom dynamics extend beyond the immediate context and the field of language learning. Among other attempts to understand, Sarah and her mentees have explored cultural differences, the religious beliefs and practices of learners, the effects of trauma on language learning, and the learners' target contexts (in the countries where they hope to be placed).

Sarah's situation is also a good reminder that researching your mentees' classroom contexts does not have to be done face-to-face. You may remember from Chapter 2 that she lives in one country while mentoring teachers in three others. When she asks questions of her mentee informants, she does so virtually. One of her favorite outside sources for exploring cultural differences is Geert Hofstede's Country Comparison page.[12] She's read books and articles about religious beliefs and the effects of trauma, and she is currently in email communication with teachers and administrators of programs that offer aid to refugees in the United States and Canada. She's shared this information and these resources with her mentees—virtually, of course—and they in turn have reported back to her on observations of and conversations with colleagues.

MENTORING IN THE CLASSROOM CONTEXT

Once you've researched your mentees' classroom dynamics, that becomes the context within which you set up your mentoring encounters. You help them down the path toward proficiency in teaching by bringing in principles and theories that fit the context. The process of learning teaching is not one of applying ideas learned in a TESOL methods course but rather choosing methods that will succeed given the inside and outside forces at work in their classrooms. Likewise, although our ideas about mentoring in this book are built around sound education principles, they may need to be adapted to fit with different contexts of mentoring. The next chapter will expand more on these contexts.

As you move on to "Now It's Your Turn" and then the next chapter, keep in mind that in addition to helping you engage in contextualized mentoring, researching your mentees' classroom dynamics has the added benefit of strengthening your relationship with them. What relationship is not made stronger by better communication and deeper understanding? Furthermore, you and your mentees may develop a clearer picture of their students' needs. This, in turn, may cycle back around to feed your curiosity and inspire you to dig deeper, honing your ability to mentor in context.

NOW IT'S YOUR TURN

The following four tasks will help you begin the process of understanding your mentees' classroom contexts. If you are currently mentoring, they are designed to be completed with your mentee informants. Otherwise they can be completed now and used as journal or support group topics and then repeated later with your mentees.

Task 4.1: Classroom Context Interview

Interview one or two of your (potential) mentees about their classroom contexts.

1. First, brainstorm a list of questions to ask. Use Figure 4.1 as a starting point. You can also use the following questions to get started:
   - How do your mentees view their roles, responsibilities, and relationships in the classroom?
   - How are their ideas different from their students?
   - What are some of the sources of these differences?
2. Your interviews can then be done informally and either face-to-face or virtually.
3. Write in your mentoring journal about what you learn, or share it in your mentor support group.

Task 4.2: Proverbs for Teachers

Compile a list of proverbs that might help you understand your current or future mentoring context.

1. Ask teachers, students, or others what proverbs are used to describe teachers' roles, responsibilities, and relationships.
2. Ask your mentees (or others) to explain what the proverbs mean and how they fit into their teaching context.
3. If the proverbs are not in your native language, ask for help translating and understanding what the proverbs mean and how they are applied to teaching and learning.
4. Write in your journal about what you learn, or share in your support group. Also talk about how you might be able to use the proverbs in future mentoring encounters with your mentees.

Task 4.3: Culture Comparison

How do/could cultural differences play a role in your mentoring? Explore how they might affect your mentees' classroom dynamics and/or your mentoring context. If you are currently mentoring, complete this task with a mentee. Otherwise, complete it on your own and use it as a journal or support group topic.

1. Use the following website to compare a current or future mentee's culture with those of their students or with yours: https://geert-hofstede.com/countries.html.
2. Design a visual (a table, chart, diagram, or picture) that shows how cultural differences could lead to tensions in the classroom or your mentoring relationship.

Task 4.4: Context Resources

Compile a list or folder of outside resources (paper, electronic, or using a file sharing system like Google Drive or Dropbox) you and your mentees might be able to draw on in order to understand their classroom contexts. If you are currently mentoring, work with your mentees on these resources. Otherwise, begin the process, keeping a record in your journal, and then finish it later with your mentees.

NOTES

1. Donald Freeman and Karen E. Johnson, "Reconceptualizing the Knowledge-Base of Language Teacher Education," *TESOL Quarterly* 32, no. 3 (1998), 397–417, https:/doi.org/10.2307/3588114.
2. H. Douglas Brown and Heekyeong Lee, *Teaching by Principles*, 4th ed. (White Plains, NY: Pearson Education, 2015).
3. Jeremy Harmer, *The Practice of English Language Teaching*, 5th ed. (Harlow: Pearson Education, 2015), 69.
4. Philida Schellekens, *The Oxford ESOL Handbook* (Oxford: Oxford University Press, 2007), 19.
5. *Collins English Dictionary Online*, s.v. "dynamics," accessed June 19, 2017, www.collinsdictionary.com/dictionary/english/dynamics.
6. Eleanor Harding, "Half of Primary Schools Set to Teach Maths Chinese-Style," *Daily Mail*, July 11, 2016, www.dailymail.co.uk/news/article-3685552/Half-primary-schools-set-teach-maths-Chinese-style-Children-required-practise-sums-exercises-prove-mastered-them.html.
7. Hunter Brimi, "Academic Instructors or Moral Guides? Moral Education in America and the Teacher's Dilemma," *The Clearinghouse: A Journal of Educational Strategies, Issues, and Ideas* 82, no. 3 (2009): 129, https:/doi.org/10.3200/TCHS.82.3.125–130.
8. Ibid., 130.
9. Craig Storti, *The Art of Crossing Cultures*, 2nd ed. (Boston: Intercultural Press, 2007).
10. Zoltan Dörnyei, *Research Methods in Applied Linguistics* (Oxford: Oxford University Press, 2007), 15.

11. Yong Zhao, "Flunking Innovation and Creativity," *The Phi Delta Kappan* 94, no. 1 (2012), 56–61, https:/doi.org/10.1177/003172171209400111.
12. "Country Comparison," *Geert Hofstede*, accessed June 22, 2017, https://geert-hofstede.com/countries.html.

REFERENCES

Brimi, Hunter. "Academic Instructors or Moral Guides? Moral Education in America and the Teacher's Dilemma." *The Clearinghouse: A Journal of Educational Strategies, Issues, and Ideas* 82, no. 3 (2009): 125–130. https:/doi.org/10.3200/TCHS.82.3.125–130.

Brown, H. Douglas and Heekyeong Lee. *Teaching by Principles*. 4th ed. White Plains, NY: Pearson Education, 2015.

"Country Comparison." *Geert Hofstede*. Accessed June 22, 2017. https://geert-hofstede.com/countries.html.

Dörnyei, Zoltan. *Research Methods in Applied Linguistics*. Oxford: Oxford University Press, 2007.

Freeman, Donald and Karen E. Johnson. "Reconceptualizing the Knowledge-Base of Language Teacher Education." *TESOL Quarterly* 32, no. 3 (1998): 397–417. https://doi.org/10.2307/3588114.

Harmer, Jeremy. *The Practice of English Language Teaching*. 5th ed. Harlow: Pearson Education, 2015.

Schellekens, Philida. *The Oxford ESOL Handbook*. Oxford: Oxford University Press, 2007.

Storti, Craig. *The Art of Crossing Cultures*. 2nd ed. Boston: Intercultural Press, 2007.

Zhao, Yong. "Flunking Innovation and Creativity." *The Phi Delta Kappan* 94, no. 1 (2012): 56–61. https:/doi.org/10.1177/003172171209400111.

CHAPTER 5

Broader Contexts of Mentoring

WHAT DO YOU THINK?

1. What is meant by being culturally aware, particularly as it relates to teaching or mentoring?
2. What cultural differences do mentors and teachers need to be aware of?
3. How can awareness of these differences be developed?
4. How can someone's attitudes or expectations interfere when crossing cultures?
5. How can teachers and mentors develop appropriate attitudes and expectations?

As you developed a clearer picture of your mentees' classroom contexts in the last chapter, you may have noted various tensions but aren't quite sure where they come from. The missing pieces, as illustrated in Figure 4.1 (Chapter 4), may come from the broader context shaping your mentees' classroom dynamics. This chapter will look at what outside forces influence your mentees' classroom contexts and in turn your mentoring context.

DEFINING CULTURAL AWARENESS

First let's see what we mean by being culturally aware. According to Risager,[1] this term "became popular within education in most anglophone parts of the world in the 1980s and 1990s." She refers to differences that may arise "from a national, ethnic, social, regional or institutional point of view." Storti[2] explains that developing awareness involves an understanding of such differences and how we react to them. Awareness, then, leads to realistic expectations and thus fewer cultural incidents. In this chapter, we are interested in raising awareness of differences in cultures, societies, education systems, and institutions that influence your mentees' classroom dynamics. We also hope to highlight the expectations you and your mentees have when crossing cultures in their classroom context and/or your mentoring relationship.

IN THEIR OWN WORDS: TRAINING TEACHERS DURING A CIVIL WAR

Nessie reflects back on an early experience in her career training teachers in a country where layers of outsides factors affected her mentoring context.

At one point in my career I was sent to train teachers of English in a country that was in the middle of a civil war. Among my roles was the mentoring of people who had already been teachers of one foreign language but who were now required to teach a different language, namely English, at the secondary school level. As time went by, I became aware of a number of interwoven cultural factors.

Starting at the national level there was the government's decision to back a different horse, *internationally speaking*. To do this, they needed the education system to change as soon as possible to English medium. The obstacles to this were clear. Hardly anyone spoke English. Very few teachers wanted to teach English. Given that the city was under attack, there was little impetus to make any changes.

The next cultural level was that of the school, where the teachers had to do their teaching practice. I use that word in the singular because all the other schools in the city continued to use and teach the other foreign language and therefore teachers of English could not complete a practicum there.

The third level which I had to work with was the most visible, namely the teachers who were sitting in front of me every day (or at least every day that acts of war didn't close things down). Some of these teachers were onto their third retraining. They had been sent abroad to countries with which theirs had enjoyed a relationship, and had come back with a love of the literature and language they had studied there. Briefly put, they were now learning to be teachers of English under duress. Other teachers in the class were much younger, having just graduated from five years at the experimental English-only high school mentioned above. Why had they gone to that school? Because their parents, as civil servants,

> had to do what they were told. Sadly, five years later these young people did not know the other foreign language which was the medium of instruction at all the university faculties. The government then solved the problem by creating a stream at the faculty of education to train teachers of English. A third group of teachers had taught in primary schools for some time and were now being rewarded for their good performance by being promoted to secondary teaching. This was not a choice.

AWARENESS OF DIFFERENCES

We would like to think that the above experience is an extreme example. However, every classroom will have layers of history, culture, and influences from local systems or education policies that affect the school's expectations of mentees. Your job as the mentor is to become aware of these "interwoven cultural factors" and the differences between you, your mentees, and their students. As an illustration, let's consider our extreme example in more detail, and we'll also return to the Chinese teacher support group (from the last chapter). Some of the questions we are using to sort through the layers are listed below.

1. Which seem more influential on your mentees' classrooms: traditions or current trends?
2. In the education system where your mentees work, what are some recent changes? How might these affect the different ways they view their roles?
3. What education and/or language policies are teachers being asked to adhere to or at least consider?
4. What metaphors do people use to describe teachers and their roles?

Training Teachers in a Civil War

One layer from "In Their Own Words: Training Teachers in a Civil War" involved changes in government policies and the reasons why languages were being taught. Historically, other foreign languages had taken precedence, but a new government made a new policy, and no matter their preferences and experiences, these teachers were required to change. English became the medium of instruction before they were ready and perhaps before their students (and parents) were willing to accept a language spoken by people previously known only as enemies. In this case, historical factors and preferences were ignored, and the classroom context was influenced by current, and largely unpleasant, events. Although some may have felt excitement about their changing roles, others were clearly disappointed, possibly frustrated, and even disillusioned. These factors were affecting their classroom context, their attitudes toward it, and potentially in turn toward learning teaching.

A Teacher Support Group in China

Prior to our support group discussions, many of the Chinese teachers had not consciously thought about the proverbs quoted in Chapter 4. Yet they could describe illustrations in either their learning or teaching experiences. In many ways, they naturally adhered to the proverbs as the way teaching had always been done. Metaphors Chinese English teachers often use to describe their roles illumine these traditions. Some of the metaphors point to their role as the source of knowledge (book) or as those who light a path toward knowledge (beacon, lighthouse, candle). Others suggest that teachers are vital to students' academic and moral development (air, water, sun) or that they are responsible for it (gardener, director). Below we've used some of our support group teachers' words to describe three of the metaphors more fully.

1. Candle: "A candle sacrifices itself to give light; a teacher disseminates knowledge and doesn't ask much in return."
2. Sun: "A teacher is like the sun because she plays the most significant role in students' growth and development. It supplies indispensable nutrition and light for the plants to grow and positive energy that encourages and inspires."
3. Gardener: "A teacher is like a gardener in that he helps to cultivate students' personality and development the same way a gardener takes care of plants."

In addition to traditional views, the teachers had also been influenced by current trends and in particular broad education reforms in China during the first decade of the 21st century. They attempted to apply the proverbs into this context, although not without difficulty. Their interest in modern trends was in part fueled by policy changes that had directed an overhaul of textbooks to follow a more communicative approach. However, the exam-based system or "exam culture" had not kept pace with these changes.[3] This contradiction sometimes caused confusion about their roles and was certainly shaping their classroom context.

Sorting the Layers

Interwoven factors shape your mentees' classroom dynamics (and in turn your mentoring context). Drawing from layers of sources, you can unweave some of these influences. The teacher support group in China, in particular, shows one way of doing this. As we suggested in the last chapter, your mentees are good cultural informants if they have been in the setting long enough. This is especially true if they are local teachers (and you the outsider) as was the case with our teacher support group. As you draw on their knowledge and experiences, they also benefit from this awareness-raising.

Another layer is the education system. One source we referred to in understanding policy changes in China was *Education for 1.3 Billion*,[4] written by a government official who oversaw many of the reforms that brought China into the 21st century. In other settings, exploring government publications together with teachers has deepened their understanding of their classroom dynamics and in turn our understanding of the mentoring context. When working with a teacher in Canada, for example, the Centre for the Canadian Language Benchmarks website[5] exposed us to the language learning standards she was expected to work toward and also gave us a larger view of her education context. The Council of Europe Language Policy Unit website[6] broadened our view of the Common European Framework of Reference for Languages and the guiding values that shape the contexts of teachers in that region. In offering support to teachers at a bilingual school in Asia where they are using curriculum and assessment tools from the United States, exploring the website for the Common Core State Standards Initiative[7] deepened both their understanding and ours.

A third layer comes from professionals and researchers working within the education system and making bridges between teachers/students, systems and cultures. *Revisiting the Chinese Learner: Changing Contexts, Changing Education*[8] made connections between classroom learning, cultural traditions, and current trends. A more recent volume, *Voices from the Frontline: Narratives of Nonnative English Speaking Teachers*,[9] has potential to bridge inside and outside forces by opening our eyes to issues inherent in being a non-native speaking English teacher in the Chinese system.

Taking a broader view, another layer of exploration is the field of English language teaching as a whole. *The Career Trajectories of English Language Teachers*,[10] for example, gives insiders' perspectives on the field from different countries around the world. From a different but still broad perspective, *English Language Education in a Global World*[11] addresses issues and trends, not necessarily limited to a particular country, at the forefront of the field.

Another broad layer you can explore is cultural differences. In the last chapter, we mentioned one of Sarah's favorite sources for investigating culture, Geert Hofstede's Country Comparison page.[12] *The Art of Crossing Cultures*[13] has raised our awareness of differences and how to manage them. *Exploring Intercultural Communication*[14] would serve the same purpose. For us, because many of the proverbs we examined with our teacher support group had roots in Confucian philosophy, we delved into some of his ancient writings. We also explored this together with mentors who were working with teachers in Confucian-heritage cultures, where the education system was in part influenced by Confucian values.[15]

> ## PUZZLE IT OUT: INTERWOVEN CHALLENGES
>
> **As Karen tries to unweave factors in her mentoring context, she describes some of the challenges she was facing with local teachers in her second culture. Excerpts from her reflections are below.**
>
> *With some teachers, no matter if the setting is more formal or more informal, from my experience, no matter how the senior teacher approaches them, they will just feel like they have very little (if anything) to offer in a dialog about improving teaching methods, classroom management, etc. Every now and then I will meet some bolder ones who are willing to stick their neck out and offer advice to other teachers.*
>
> *It so often comes back to these kinds of things: "Teacher, tell me HOW to fix this problem and the challenge I have!" Once I give them my suggestions and/or lead them in a dialog to consider possible solutions, I often get one of two responses: "Yes, okay, BUT . . ." OR "Hmmm . . . I see, yes, I understand, that sounds good" (but then when they go home they are not willing to try the advice I've given them).*
>
> *I am convinced more and more that so much of it comes back to the root of the issue: changing the way I think, and someone else changing the way he/she thinks . . . I am not saying that I want to turn the teachers into Western Psychology students . . . I simply mean that it would be nice to reach some middle ground. I am happy to try to adapt myself to a certain degree cross-culturally (for example, giving some prescriptive advice as the expert even when that can make me feel authoritative and uncomfortable personally, because that is what they expect), but I would also like to see these teachers both gain confidence in themselves and also learn to think in a way that will help them solve classroom/lesson problems successfully when we are no longer there to mentor them and answer their questions.*

BROADER CONTEXTS OF MENTORING 77

> *It has struck me again and perhaps more acutely—that I am really being pulled in three different directions. There is the way my faith tells me to live, act, teach, and mentor; there is the way my culture tells me to do these things; and there is the way my host culture tells me to do these things. I'm beginning to think that it is really a rare instance when all three of these directions really intersect. Yet I live in this tension.*

WHAT DO YOU THINK?

1. What layers of factors seemed to be influencing Karen's mentoring context?
2. How might these layers have also influenced her mentees' teaching contexts?
3. What could Karen and her mentees do in order to sort out some of these layers? In other words, how could they raise their awareness of some of the differences?
4. What personal factors also came into play? How did they seem to be causing confusion and possibly even conflict?
5. What could Karen and her mentees do in order to resolve confusion and/or conflict?

AWARENESS OF SELF

As you are developing, in tandem with your mentees, an awareness of interwoven factors, it is also important to raise your self-awareness. This means that you and your mentees reflect on your expectations and attitudes when crossing contextual boundaries. Storti[16] explains that cultural incidents occur not as a result of differences but because of our beliefs. We expect others to act, think, and feel as we do, and when they don't, we are likely to react negatively (or they will) giving rise to confusion and even conflict. The solution is to become aware of our reactions, reflect on their sources, and develop appropriate expectations.

The starting point for self-awareness may be values that we first introduced in Chapter 2. There the focus was on your mentees. Here, we want to draw you into the picture and suggest that not only is teaching an inherently "value-laden activity"[17] but so also is mentoring. Johnston's recommendation that each teacher "examine her own values and beliefs about what is good and right for her own learners"[18] applies to mentors as well. This seems to be where Karen was headed in her reflections. In order to mentor well, she was exploring potential cultural differences. At the same time, she was wondering about personal beliefs and recognizing a need to let go.

Johnston lists three categories of moral dilemmas that you and your mentees may want to consider as you examine your attitudes and expectations.

Pedagogy

Pedagogy is, of course, just the technical term for ways of teaching. One of the dilemmas Johnston lists under this heading is evaluation and its necessity versus the impossibility of measuring students' ability/progress in ways that are fully fair. The teachers in our support group face this dilemma every day when using textbooks designed to take a communicative approach but within a system where exams primarily measure students' ability to manipulate forms. Both the teachers and we the mentors may hold to a full range of beliefs about the fairness of such a contradiction and how to teach (toward the exam or by the textbook). The teachers may need help raising their awareness of the dilemma and their attitudes toward it. Two questions that come to mind as mentors in this context are: (1) As an outsider, how can I both be sympathetic to the teachers' situation and respect the system? (2) Should I be helping teachers look for ways to change the system or teach within it?

Teacher-Student Relationships

The dilemmas under this heading echo tensions in the last chapter related to authority and learner autonomy: (1) how to maintain authority in the classroom in culturally appropriate ways while still encouraging "solidarity" with the students,[19] and (2) how far a teacher is responsible for each student's learning. Your mentees who are crossing cultures in the classroom may need to reflect on their expectations before finding an appropriate balance. Furthermore, when you are crossing contextual boundaries in the mentoring relationship, you too may need some self-examination and letting go so that, like Karen, you can "reach some middle ground."

Beliefs and Values

In this third category, Johnston speaks of politics, personal faith, tolerance, and professionalism. As we've stated in previous chapters, these are topics that may be difficult for you even to broach because they can evoke strong feelings that can blind us to other perspectives. You, like Karen, may feel pulled in different directions as you "live in this tension."

Johnston's word "complexity"[20] says it all. Still, the fact that answers are not easy need not stop you from considering how these points might affect your mentees' classroom contexts and your mentoring relationship.

MENTORING IN BROADER CONTEXTS

Complexity is, in fact, a good word to describe mentoring in context. Interwoven forces make up your mentees' classroom dynamics and your mentoring context. Sorting the threads may involve exploring layers of resources while at the same time recognizing how personal beliefs and values influence attitudes and expectations. Unweaving these factors, in collaboration with your mentees, may resolve tensions. As they teach you about their contexts and you explore outside forces together, the process also becomes another layer in facilitative mentoring.

NOW IT'S YOUR TURN

The tasks below will help you understand the broad contexts of mentoring. Tasks 5.1 and 5.3 assume that you are currently mentoring. Alternatively, you could complete them by talking to potential mentees or others in your future mentoring context (teachers, students, or administrators). Then, in your mentoring journal or mentor support group, reflect on what you learn. Task 5.2 follows up on a task in Chapter 4.

Task 5.1: Exploring Interwoven Factors

Explore some of the interwoven influences on your mentee's classroom dynamics. First, compile a list of questions to help you sort through the layers. You can use the questions below (from earlier in the chapter) as a starting point. Then, work with your mentee to pose other questions, find answers, and identify areas you may need to explore further.

1. Which seem more influential on your mentees' classrooms: traditions or current trends?
2. In the education system where your mentees work, what are some recent changes? How might these affect the different ways they view their roles?
3. What education and/or language policies are teachers being asked to adhere to or at least consider?
4. What metaphors do people use to describe teachers and their roles?

Task 5.2: Context Resources

In Task 4.4, you had an opportunity to compile resources to help you and your mentees understand their classroom contexts. Add to that list with resources for further exploring areas you identified in Task 5.1. Resources listed in this chapter may be a good starting point.

Task 5.3: Developing Self-Awareness

Using Table 5.1 below as a template, work with your mentees to reflect on expectations and attitudes toward learning and teaching (theirs, their students', and yours). Then, drawing on what you've learned in Task 5.1

Table 5.1 **Developing Self-Awareness**

		Students	Teacher	Mentor	Analysis
Pedagogy	Form vs. function				
	Ways of evaluating				
	Process vs. product				
Teacher-Student Relationships	Learner autonomy				
	Authority				
Values and Beliefs	Politics				
	Faith				
	Professionalism				

and resources you collected for 5.2, analyze some of the differences. In addition to reasons related to culture, education systems, and institutions, what personal values influence your attitudes and expectations? (The subcategories in the table are selected from Johnston.)[21]

NOTES

1. Karen Risager, "Cultural Awareness," in *Routledge Encyclopedia of Language Teaching and Learning*, 2nd ed., ed. Michael Byram and Adelheid Hu (London and New York: Routledge, 2013), 181.
2. Craig Storti, *The Art of Crossing Cultures*, 2nd ed. (Boston: Intercultural Press, 2007).
3. Chunmei Yan, "'We Can't Change Much Unless the Exams Change': Teachers' Dilemmas in the Curriculum Reform in China," *Improving Schools* 18, no. 1 (2015): 14, https:/doi.org/10.1177/1365480214553744.
4. Lanqing Li, *Education for 1.3 Billion* (Beijing: Foreign Language Teaching and Research Press and Pearson Education, 2004).
5. *Centre for Canadian Language Benchmarks*, accessed June 22, 2017, www.language.ca/index.cfm?Repertoire_No=2137991327.
6. "Education and Languages, Language Policy," *Council of Europe*, accessed June 22, 2017, www.coe.int/t/dg4/linguistic/.
7. *Common Core State Standards Initiative*, accessed June 22, 2017, www.corestandards.org/.
8. Carol K. K. Chan and Nirmala Rao, eds., *Revisiting the Chinese Learner: Changing Contexts, Changing Education* (Hong Kong: Comparative Education Research Centre, 2009).
9. Icy Lee and Paul Sze, *Voices from the Frontline: Narratives of Nonnative English Speaking Teachers* (Hong Kong: Chinese University Press, 2015).
10. Penny Haworth and Cheryl Craig, eds., *The Career Trajectories of English Language Teachers* (Oxford: Symposium Books, 2016), https:/doi.org/10.15730/books.97.
11. Lap Tuen Wong and Aditi Dubey-Jhaveri, eds., *English Language Education in a Global World: Practices, Issues and Challenges* (New York: Nova Science Publishers, 2015), https:/doi.org/10.131401/RG.2.1.4479.1129.
12. "Country Comparison," *Geert Hofstede*, accessed June 22, 2017, https://geert-hofstede.com/countries.html.
13. Storti, *The Art of Crossing Cultures*.
14. Zhu Hua, *Exploring Intercultural Communication: Language in Action* (London: Routledge, 2014).
15. Chan and Rao, *Revisiting the Chinese Learner*.
16. Storti, *The Art of Crossing Cultures*.
17. Bill Johnston, *Values in English Language Teaching* (Mahwah, NJ: Lawrence Erlbaum Associates Publishers, 2003), Kindle edition, chap. 1.
18. Ibid., chap. 7.
19. Ibid.
20. Ibid.
21. Ibid.

REFERENCES

Centre for Canadian Language Benchmarks. Accessed June 22, 2017. www.language.ca/index.cfm?Repertoire_No=2137991327.

Chan, Carol K. K. and Nirmala Rao, eds. *Revisiting the Chinese Learner: Changing Contexts, Changing Education.* Hong Kong: Comparative Education Research Centre, 2009.

Common Core State Standards Initiative. Accessed June 22, 2017. www.corestandards.org/.

"Country Comparison." *Geert Hofstede.* Accessed June 22, 2017. https://geert-hofstede.com/countries.html.

"Education and Languages, Language Policy." *Council of Europe.* Accessed June 22, 2017. www.coe.int/t/dg4/linguistic/.

Haworth, Penny and Cheryl Craig, eds. *The Career Trajectories of English Language Teachers.* Oxford: Symposium Books, 2016. https:/doi.org/10.15730/books.97.

Hua, Zhu. *Exploring Intercultural Communication: Language in Action.* London: Routledge, 2014.

Johnston, Bill. *Values in English Language Teaching.* Mahwah, NJ: Lawrence Erlbaum Associates Publishers, 2003. Kindle edition.

Lee, Icy and Paul Sze. *Voices from the Frontline: Narratives of Nonnative English Speaking Teachers.* Hong Kong: Chinese University Press, 2015.

Li, Lanqing. *Education for 1.3 Billion.* Beijing: Foreign Language Teaching and Research Press and Pearson Education, 2004.

Risager, Karen. "Cultural Awareness." In *Routledge Encyclopedia of Language Teaching and Learning.* 2nd ed., edited by Michael Byram and Adelheid Hu, 181–184. London and New York: Routledge, 2013.

Storti, Craig. *The Art of Crossing Cultures.* 2nd ed. Boston: Intercultural Press, 2007.

Wong, Lap Tuen and Aditi Dubey-Jhaveri, eds. *English Language Education in a Global World: Practices, Issues and Challenges.* New York: Nova Science Publishers, 2015. https:/doi.org/10.131401/RG.2.1.4479.1129.

Yan, Chunmei. "'We Can't Change Much Unless the Exams Change': Teachers' Dilemmas in the Curriculum Reform in China." *Improving Schools* 18, no. 1 (2015): 5–19. https:/doi.org/10.1177/1365480214553744.

SECTION III
Interactive Mentoring

Those are really good questions. Sometimes questions are suggestions, aren't they?
—a mentee talking to her mentor

I felt like communication with my mentees was disjointed and it was hard to keep track of what I had said to whom.
—Tracy

I'm always sure to include helpful information (regarding culture or theory that may influence the success of a lesson), questions that will cause the teachers to think about previous conversations or the coursework done during training and assess portions of their plan accordingly or simply celebrate growth and success in creating activities that are well thought out and reflect the stated course goals.
—Cheryl

CHAPTER 6

Challenges to Effective Communication

WHAT DO YOU THINK?

1. What are some of the challenges a mentor may face when interacting with mentees?
2. What role do feelings play in mentoring and being mentored?
3. How important is mentor input in mentoring interactions? How important is mentee output? How can you find a balance between the two?
4. How might virtual mentoring solve or exacerbate some of the challenges in mentoring interactions?

An employee was sharing a personal challenge with her employer. Recognizing her own tendency to jump in with advice, the employer was trying instead to listen and ask good questions. After putting some effort into responding, the employee said, "Those are really good questions. Sometimes questions are suggestions, aren't they?"

The employer later reflected on this conversation and why her questions came across as advice. She had been trying to interact with her employee in a way that led toward autonomy. However, does she still need to work on her communication skills, or is it possible that the conversation went exactly as it should have, and it was in and through the interaction that learning occurred?

One view of learning that fits well with mentoring is sociocultural theory, which sees "teaching and learning as social rather than individual."[1] Learning occurs "when problems are solved by novices and experts working together"[2] in the learner's Zone of Proximal Development (ZPD), which includes the knowledge and skills s/he is able to acquire but only

86   INTERACTIVE MENTORING

with the help of a "guide" or "advisor."[3] The gap between a teacher's "actual" and "potential" progress could be described as a her/his ZPD.[4] The process of traversing the ZPD requires some scaffolding, which could come in the form of help from a mentor who is further along the path. In this case, learning occurs as mentor and mentee negotiate and collaboratively make progress toward where the mentee needs to be. As our opening illustration suggests, these interactions can present challenges. In this chapter, we'll talk about some of those challenges. Then, Chapters 7 and 8 respond to the challenges with some ways to engage in interactive mentoring effectively.

MANAGING AFFECTIVE CONCERNS

For many teachers who have been around the field of language teaching a while, the term *affective filter* flows in and out of conversations. You may have talked about lowering your students' affective filters so that negative emotions do not interfere with language learning or use. In interactions between mentors and mentees, we could also talk about an affective filter. For our mentors in training and others, affective concerns play an important role in their mentoring interactions. They endeavor to avoid words and circumstances in which their mentees feel "a personal sense of failure and the appearance of failure in front of the students."[5] They try to turn "a sense of threat into trust"[6] and "provide feedback that is affirming, non-threatening, and, at the same time, effective."[7]

What is interesting about the mentoring affective filter is that it has an influence on both mentors and mentees. In chapter 1, you read about how some mentors may fluctuate between feeling confident and novice-like. Many of our mentors in training have tried to alleviate affective concerns for their mentees, but they also worry about exacerbating them by being too forthright or coming across as judgmental. For some mentors, their concerns about their mentees' feelings cause their own affective filter to go up.

HERE'S WHAT HAPPENED: FACTORS INFLUENCING THE AFFECTIVE FILTER

As the employer in the opening illustration has developed her mentoring skills (in the office and with teachers), she has been exposed to a variety of factors that influence the affective filter. A few of her experiences are recounted below.

> In the mentor's interactions with American teachers, two contrasting experiences stand out. In one, after noting that a teacher's students seemed inattentive and off task during class, she started the follow-up conversation with this question, "How did you feel about today's class?" Immediately the teacher began to cry. In the second, at the end of an intensive two days observing a teacher and giving both positive and carefully worded negative feedback, the teacher said, "You've given me a lot of encouragement. I wish you would tell me some things I could work on."
>
> Once the mentor was invited to sit in on a practice MA thesis defense in China. After completing their presentations, the three students left the room. During the ensuing discussion, the professor in charge said, "They all did a good job, but let's not tell them that. Otherwise, they'll stop working, and they still have a month left before their final defense." This experience seemed to emphasize something she had recently read. In *The Geography of Thought*,[8] Nisbett, in his admittedly broad generalizations, describes an Asian quest for self-improvement versus a Western concern for self-esteem.
>
> Expatriates living in China are occasionally taken aback by unsolicited advice. They may be offered suggestions from friends, students, and random strangers about their appearance or teaching techniques. They may also receive text messages from friends on the first cold day of winter reminding them to wear long underwear. This mentor once asked her Chinese graduate students in a pragmatics course to analyze interactions like these and why Americans might feel uncomfortable and even insulted. Although one student suggested that any negative reactions to advice were "arrogant," others explained more mildly, "This is how we show care and concern for each other."

WHAT DO YOU THINK?

1. What factors might be playing into this mentor's understanding of the affective filter in mentoring encounters?
2. What factors might influence her own?
3. What factors might play into your own understanding of the affective filter (yours and your mentees') in mentoring encounters?

In the last two chapters, we touched on some personal and cultural factors that influence your mentoring context. These factors also come into play when trying to figure out your mentee's affect. Too much praise, especially if it is not genuine (or even if it is simply perceived that way), or feedback given too gently can have an unintended result. Rather than lowering the affective filter, it may cause some teachers to feel that they are not receiving what they need. On the other hand, hearing where and how they are succeeding may offer relief to people who are feeling anxious about teaching or being mentored. Furthermore, when you take the time both to help and learn how to interact in appropriate ways, your mentees may feel cared for. Whether trying to communicate positive or negative feedback, *apt* seems to be a good word to describe how to interact with your mentees in a way that meets their affective needs. The next chapter will expand on this, but in brief, *apt* interactions use words and techniques that suit the circumstances and fit each mentee personally and culturally. In the process, your own affective filter is lowered.

BALANCING INPUT AND OUTPUT

Sometimes the interaction between mentor and mentee is described as *giving* advice or *offering* feedback. However, the interaction is not as one-sided as these terms suggest. Traversing the ZPD is done as problems are solved together. As Asa expressed it (Chapter 4), mentoring is collaboration—co-planning, co-teaching, and co-development. As both parties negotiate the meaning of teaching, progress can be made toward proficiency and also the ultimate goal of autonomy. In other words, mentees need both to receive input and produce output.

Another term that has become part of a language teacher's vernacular, $i + 1$, helps to describe the type of input teachers need. As Brown[9] points out, this idea that input should be one step beyond learners' current level is simply a reiteration of what happens in the ZPD. In your mentoring encounters, $i + 1$ is advice from you that is scaffolded or takes teachers step by step across the ZPD to where they can and need to be. In mentoring interactions, however, appropriate input is not only comprehensible but also draws mentees down the path toward both teaching proficiency and reflection and self-evaluation. Moreover, it is apt so that, affectively, mentees can receive it and put it to use.

For mentees, output is not simply internalized input that emerges in their teaching. It too leads toward awareness and learner ownership. A tool for understanding your mentees' output might be a Bloom's Taxonomy for Mentoring, illustrated in Figure 6.1. Since its creation, Bloom's Taxonomy has been used in many educational settings. Here we adapt it to mentoring interactions. There are many different ways to refer to and represent Bloom's Taxonomy. Figure 6.1 draws on the revised version[10] and views the six levels (highlighted in the figure) from surface to deep. We've also

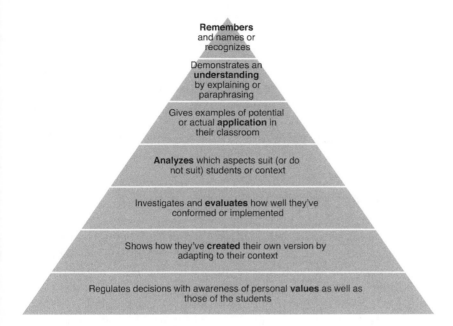

Figure 6.1 Bloom's Taxonomy for Mentoring

added a seventh level in order to reflect discussions in other parts of this book. (An online search of "Bloom's Revised Taxonomy" will take you to sites with information about both the original and revised versions.)

Here's how a Bloom's Taxonomy for Mentoring might work where the goal is to encourage mentees down the taxonomy toward evaluation and ownership. Consider situations where a principle or technique from a TESOL (Teaching English to Speakers of Other Language) methods course comes up in your mentoring interactions. At the surface, your mentees show that they remember and understand. They, then, can give an example or demonstrate how the idea works in the classroom. Going deeper, they are able to analyze how well it fits into their context (or doesn't) and reflectively evaluate how well they've done at making use of it. Finally, they tell you (and perhaps you also see) how they are able to put it into practice in the classroom by taking ownership of it. In mentoring that delves into a *values* dimension, your mentees, with awareness of their moral agency in the classroom, may need to go one step further and make decisions that reflect their values while also respecting those of their students.

When you're trying to find a balance between input and output, think of your mentoring interactions as having the usual give and take of everyday conversations. They are dialogs not monologs.[11] Of course, personal and cultural factors come into play here. The employee in our opening illustration, for example, may have expected more advice than her employer was giving so much so that she assumed the questions were input. However, allowing for inside and outside forces does not mean you're stuck at a particular point. They simply tell you where to begin so that your mentees are affectively in a good place. Then, traversing the ZPD, in addition to guiding toward teaching proficiency, is slowly challenging them to engage in more reflective dialog.

FACE-TO-FACE VS. VIRTUAL INTERACTIONS

Your first thought when you read this heading may be that mentoring in virtual settings exacerbates the challenges listed above. Let's return to Steve's situation, which was first introduced in Chapter 1. His first choice would have been face-to-face mentoring, but having been forced into a virtual setting, he experienced both complications and possibilities. Notice in particular what he says about affect and input in his reflections below.

IN THEIR OWN WORDS: USING A BLOG FOR INTERACTIVE MENTORING

In order to mentor teachers living in a different country, Steve set up a blog. Following each of his posts, he gave participants a task (like observing or interviewing a local teacher). Once completed, each mentee posted a report and then engaged in discussion about each other's experiences.

A blog has the potential of being an excellent tool for teacher mentoring. Since the medium is somewhat non-confrontational it allows the mentor to address important issues directly without the mentees feeling attacked. One drawback of this is that it is difficult to address a variety of issues that are specific to a variety of mentee needs.

Listening and digestion are important parts of mentoring. One advantage of the blog is that it allows the mentee to digest input over time and at their own pace. For the mentor, the pace of the blog allows for some focused thought put into written words over time. This is in contrast to the real-time thoughts mentors must deliver in face to face meetings with mentees.

In some cases of face-to-face mentoring the mentee may feel threatened or defensive when receiving feedback. This affective hurdle can inhibit digestion of important information from the mentor. In the case of the blog, the mentee not only has the time and distance to receive feedback, but they also have the opportunity to display their comprehension by writing a response or completing an assignment. The written record of the blog and potential online conversation on the blog allows for an opportunity for both the mentor and mentee to refer back to information. This is quite different than face-to-face verbal meetings when both mentor and mentee must rely on their memory of a discussion and rarely get the chance to refer back to exactly what was said. The drawback here is that at times mentees can hide behind the curtain of cyberspace and perhaps not reveal their true selves. The mentoring blog works well when teachers are transparent. The mentor must rely on the honesty and self-awareness of the mentee in order to address their needs.

In terms of accountability the blog does have the drawback of feeling distant and perhaps less of a priority since it is not a physical person talking to you. Unless the participants in the blog have a strong intrinsic motivation or a strong relationship with the other mentees, there is potential for a lack of momentum and community in an online discussion. Although the responses in the discussion have the potential of being more articulate, the participation in a discussion can be lacking since the virtual community feels distant.

As the author of the blog I really enjoyed the exercise of writing and the idea that I could reach a group of people in a variety of contexts and countries. If we would have had more possible participants I think it would have been a great means of mentoring. I enjoyed the fact that I could invest my time in the blog at my own schedule as this fits in with my current obligations.

WHAT DO YOU THINK?

1. In what ways did Steve's virtual interactions help him overcome affective barriers? How did it exacerbate them?
2. In what ways did Steve's virtual interactions provide opportunities for both input and output? What limitations do you see?
3. How might virtual interactions help or hinder reflective dialog?

Although there are obvious drawbacks to virtual interactions not least of which is motivation or buy-in, Steve found some advantages in his context. The pace, for example, afforded time and opportunity for him to offer apt input and for his mentees to "digest" it. Moreover, the distance lessened the potential for face threat because of the "non-confrontational" nature of the blog. Steve also notes that the medium made it possible for his mentees to "display comprehension." In addition to providing a memory aid, the written record (more easily than a face-to-face interaction) could be analyzed using Bloom's Taxonomy for Mentoring, and then Steve could decide how to draw his mentees deeper if necessary.

TOWARD AUTONOMOUS LEARNING

Good interactions, free of affective issues, between you and your mentees can smooth the journey across the ZPD. Moreover, because the path leads both to teaching proficiency and learner ownership, whether you are mentoring face-to-face or virtually, a balance between input and output is important. Your mentees need to engage in reflective dialog so as to become learners of teaching. The tasks in "Now It's Your Turn" guide you to lay a foundation for better mentoring interactions. Then, Chapters 7 and 8 will take you further and deeper.

NOW IT'S YOUR TURN

Task 6.1: A Mentoring Affective Filter

How might a mentoring affective filter play a role in your current or future mentoring interactions? Reflect on this question in your mentoring journal by writing your own "In Your Own Words" or "Here's What Happened." You can use the questions below to get started. Then, in your mentor support group, take turns sharing your reflections or vignettes and deciding on appropriate steps.

1. How do affective issues influence the way you interact with mentees?
   - Do you feel confident about communicating with them, or do you feel like a novice?
   - Do you have a fear of sounding judgmental or coming across as too forthright?
   - How do past interactions with your own mentors (or supervisors) influence your feelings about giving advice?
   - What other personal or cultural factors influence your feelings about giving advice?
2. How do affective issues influence the way your (potential) mentees feel about their interactions with you?

- How might past experiences and other personal factors influence their feelings?
- What cultural factors may come into play?

3. What steps do you need to take in order to facilitate apt interactions with your (potential) mentees?
    - How much praise should you give, and what type?
    - Do you need to be more direct or less? More or less gentle?
    - What would cause your mentees to feel cared for and better your mentoring relationships?
    - Would a virtual medium be a help or a hindrance?

Task 6.2: Balancing Input and Output

Record an interaction between a mentor and mentee or look at a written record (from an email, for example). This could be an interaction between a mentee and you or another mentor (with permission). Use the questions below to guide you as you write in your journal or discuss the interaction with your support group.

1. What balance between input and output do you see? Does it seem appropriate?
2. What type of mentee output is there? Use Bloom's Taxonomy for Mentoring to analyze the output.
3. How does the mode (face-to-face or virtual) influence the balance between input and output or the type of mentee output?
4. How do you think the mentor should guide the next interaction with the mentee?

NOTES

1. Kathleen M. Bailey, "Language Teacher Supervision," in *The Cambridge Guide to Second Language Teacher Education*, ed. Anne Burns and Jack C. Richards (Cambridge: Cambridge University Press, 2009), Kindle edition, chap. 27.
2. Ibid.
3. Mick Randall and Barbara Thornton, *Advising and Supporting Teachers* (Cambridge: Cambridge University Press, 2001), 52.
4. Ibid., 70.
5. Melissa K. Smith and Marilyn Lewis, "The Language Teaching Practicum: Perspectives from Mentors," *The Teacher Trainer* 23, no. 2 (2009): 7.
6. Melissa K. Smith and Marilyn Lewis, "Toward Facilitative Mentoring and Catalytic Interventions," *ELT Journal* 69, no. 2 (2015): 11, https://doi.org/10.1093/elt/ccu075.

7. Christopher Stillwell, "The Collaborative Development of Teacher Training Skills," *ELT Journal* 63, no. 4 (2009): 358, https:/doi.org/10.1093/elt/ccn068.
8. Richard E. Nisbett, *The Geography of Thought* (New York: Free Press, 2003), Kindle edition.
9. H. Douglas Brown and Heekyeong Lee, *Teaching by Principles*, 4th ed. (White Plains, NY: Pearson Education, 2015).
10. David R. Krathwohl, "A Revision of Bloom's Taxonomy: An Overview," *Theory into Practice* 41, no. 4 (2002), 212–218, https:/doi.org/10.15730/books.97.
11. Ewen Arnold, "Assessing the Quality of Mentoring: Sinking or Learning to Swim," *ELT Journal* 60, no. 2 (2006), 117–124, https:/doi.org/10.1093/elt/cci098.

REFERENCES

Arnold, Ewen. "Assessing the Quality of Mentoring: Sinking or Learning to Swim." *ELT Journal* 60, no. 2 (2006): 117–124. https:/doi.org/10.1093/elt/cci098.
Bailey, Kathleen M. "Language Teacher Supervision." In *The Cambridge Guide to Second Language Teacher Education*, edited by Anne Burns and Jack C. Richards, Chapter 27. Cambridge: Cambridge University Press, 2009. Kindle edition.
Brown, H. Douglas and Heekyeong Lee. *Teaching by Principles*. 4th ed. White Plains, NY: Pearson Education, 2015.
Krathwohl, David R. "A Revision of Bloom's Taxonomy: An Overview." *Theory into Practice* 41, no. 4 (2002): 212–218. https:/doi.org/10.15730/books.97.
Nisbett, Richard E. *The Geography of Thought*. New York: Free Press, 2003. Kindle edition.
Randall, Mick and Barbara Thornton. *Advising and Supporting Teachers*. Cambridge: Cambridge University Press, 2001.
Smith, Melissa K. and Marilyn Lewis. "The Language Teaching Practicum: Perspectives from Mentors." *The Teacher Trainer* 23, no. 2 (2009): 5–8.
Smith, Melissa K. and Marilyn Lewis. "Toward Facilitative Mentoring and Catalytic Interventions." *ELT Journal* 69, no. 2 (2015): 140–150. https:/doi.org/10.1093/elt/ccu075.
Stillwell, Christopher. "The Collaborative Development of Teacher Training Skills." *ELT Journal* 63, no. 4 (2009): 353–362. https:/doi.org/10.1093/elt/ccn068.

CHAPTER 7

The Mentor's Feedback Role

WHAT DO YOU THINK?

1. What do teachers picture when they hear the word feedback?
2. What are some different ways you have received feedback?
3. What methods of giving feedback seem to work best?
4. How do personal and cultural factors affect feedback interactions?

Ask any teacher what a mentor does, and many will list observing and giving feedback. As you participate in this book, we hope your view is growing to include more than those two aspects of mentoring. That is not to say that feedback is unimportant. In fact, one of the primary roles you will engage in is giving advice whether on lesson plans, in post-observation discussions, during support groups, or on action research projects.

Feedback is often what causes the affective issues we introduced in the last chapter, for both mentee and mentor. Moreover, giving advice is where mentors often struggle to find a balance between input and output or between monolog and dialog. In fact, as Malderez[1] points out in a note at the end of her chapter on mentoring, the term *giving feedback* is in itself problematic because it suggests one-way transmission rather than a collaborative interaction.

This chapter focusses on feedback as one important aspect of interactive mentoring. After talking about modes of communication, we offer advice on how to *give* feedback. You'll see a feedback continuum and a variety styles and begin to think about different ways of determining your approach.

MODES OF COMMUNICATION

Thinking back on your mentoring experiences, you may picture feedback as notes handwritten on a lesson plan or observation form or more formally typed on paper or in an email. Whether one-way or collaborative, you also likely remember face-to-face post-observation conferences. However, feedback, can take many forms. A few years ago, one of our mentors in training followed up his face-to-face feedback with a one-page letter to each teacher and then invited email dialog.[2] More recently, Sarah and Steve have used email and Skype to discuss planning and teaching issues with mentees in their multi-country setting in the Middle East. Anna and Ben followed up on workshops and support group meetings by using WeChat, a social media platform familiar to their teachers in China. Then, in their US setting, they engaged teachers in discussions through the comments sections on their blog. Steve's blog included both formal interactions (posts) and more informal feedback (commenting).

In today's technologically savvy world, you have many choices for communication with your mentees, more than we've listed and likely more than you need. In Chapter 3, you read about the organizational challenges Tracy faced in setting up an online forum. Here you read about other struggles she had related to choosing modes of communication.

IN THEIR OWN WORDS: DISTANCE MENTORING AND MODES OF COMMUNICATION

In order to complete an assignment for a course on mentoring, Tracy set up an online forum to supplement other modes of communication she was using to distance mentor two new expatriate teachers in China. By inviting others to participate, she hoped to "deepen discussions" and "build a professional community" involving both novice and veteran teachers.

[This] leads to the first realization I have about using a [Google Groups] forum as a mentoring or professional development tool. Between email, Skype/Facetime conversations, and the forum, I felt like communication with my mentees was disjointed and it was hard to keep track of what I had said to whom. Perhaps in the future the forum could be in the place of something else, but trying to keep up with all three did not work well for me. I acknowledge the problem could be with me, but to use a forum well, I think it would be more efficient to provide more structure to what kind of communication (questions, resource-sharing, insights to the universe at large) happens in which format. I was getting questions by email

> and Skype, and the forum was largely ignored as a means of asking questions by the mentees with little or no shared teaching insights within the group.
> In recent emails with Anna, she gave me an idea for an alternate method: to use WeChat to create a group. The immediacy of WeChat could alleviate the delay that Google Groups imposed. To get to Google Groups, most mentees in China would need to use a computer/VPN client, and would expect a bit of delay until the moderator could do likewise. In contrast, WeChat would ping a moderator's phone and could be replied to fairly quickly. I've heard that WeChat can also be used to make verbal messages, send files, link to websites, and incorporate photos.[3] I have to admit, I don't know how to do some of those things with WeChat, so there would be a learning curve, but it would be possible to accomplish many of the same things Google Groups can do with a locally-produced software and increase the speed and the likelihood of participation.

WHAT DO YOU THINK?

1. What were some of the struggles Tracy had in choosing modes of communication for her mentoring?
2. Which of her solutions might you choose?
3. How could the struggles or solutions affect her feedback interactions with mentees?
4. What are some of the factors you would like to keep in mind as you make your choices?

With all the options available, how do you choose? Sometimes the decision is made for you, at least to a certain extent. Tracy lives in a different city from her mentees, Sarah and Steve in a different country. They have no option but an online format. We've been flown into a city to spend a few days working intensively with mentees, seemingly with no choice but face-to-face feedback. Anna and Ben mentored their colleagues face-to-face but chose to supplement with follow-up feedback in a virtual setting. Whether you're choosing between virtual and face-to-face or making narrower decisions about how to work within the mode you've been assigned, here are some lessons gleaned from the experiences of Tracy, Steve (See "In Their Own Words: Using a Blog for Interactive Mentoring," Chapter 6), and other mentors.

A Variety of Modes

Using more than one mode could be helpful for your mentees. If you're coming into the setting from the outside, for example, you may want to lay some groundwork in a virtual setting prior to your arrival. If the affective filter becomes an issue in face-to-face feedback, a virtual follow up may provide a non-threatening environment in which to continue, or it may give you and your mentees time to digest and respond more thoughtfully. A follow up using a different mode may also clarify, reinforce, or lead to further discussion. However, too much variety could overwhelm your mentees, or as Tracy experienced, you could confuse yourself.

Convenience

Consider what is most accessible to you and your mentees. When you're nearby or someone else is willing to pay for travel, face-to-face is an option. When choosing virtual modes, requiring your mentees to use a new program or application could be burdensome unless perhaps it could become an appropriate teaching tool. (However, this does not preclude you from learning *their* technology as Tracy was willing to do.) Moreover, if mentees have to go to too much effort, like first accessing a VPN[4] in a country that blocks certain programs, they may choose not to participate.

Also consider what fits teachers' lifestyles. In a subsequent conversation, Tracy pointed out that another hurdle for her mentees was sitting down in front of their computers. In a world where cellphones have become an extension of our arms and immediate is the norm, using a platform accessible on their phones, one they were already using, made more sense.

Establishing Relationship

No matter what mode you choose (or are assigned), you will need to figure out how to establish a genuine and collaborative relationship within which to hold feedback interactions. Each mode comes with its own challenges. As Steve pointed out, virtual modes can make a relationship seem distant and lack collaboration. When we've been flown in for intensive mentoring stints, we've had to look for ways to establish the relationship and alleviate a sense of threat with, for instance, online communication prior to our visit or an informal chat over tea upon our arrival.

Register and Rules of Politeness

Pragmatics for Feedback below will go into more detail, but first let's think through some of the challenges when switching between face-to-face and virtual communication. Consider, for example, about how a received message doesn't always match your intent, how non-verbal cues (tone and facial expression) play a role in getting your intent across, and how to communicate tone and intent in an email or another online format. Also consider formality and how much is appropriate in your feedback interactions. Regardless of your mode of communication, what level of professionalism is appropriate? How do you maintain it, on social media, for example, which is by nature informal?

TYPES OF FEEDBACK

Regardless of what modes of communication you settle on, you are also faced with choices about what types of interaction are appropriate. Let's consider two models of feedback that our mentors in training have found helpful. The first is a continuum, the second a framework.

The Directive to Facilitative Continuum

Earlier in the book, we described mentoring on a continuum ranging from directive to facilitative. This continuum is specifically applicable to your mentoring interactions. Malderez[5] describes a range from "'mentor'-delivered judgements to more collaborative discussions." Instead of mentor monologs, Arnold suggests aiming for "reflective dialogue."[6] Randall and Thornton use the word "authoritative" rather than directive.[7] They also describe adviser vs. teacher-directed communication.[8] In his study of mentor training, Stillwell[9] shows how mentee-controlled interactions are more collaborative and also more likely to lead to learner ownership. Some of these words and others like them are used to illustrate the two ends of the continuum in Figure 7.1.

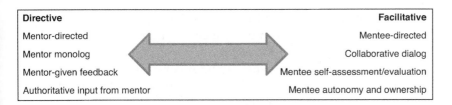

Figure 7.1 Directive to Facilitative Feedback

The Intervention Framework

In his framework, Heron describes six categories of intervention whereby "practitioners" offer words that lead their "clients" toward personal

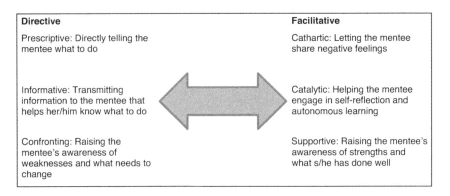

Figure 7.2 Intervention Framework

growth.[10] He applied it to a wide range of settings including education and training. Randall and Thornton[11] put it into the context of mentoring interactions and show how the two broader categories of intervention, authoritative and facilitative, fit a mentor's advice-giving role. Although Heron and Randall and Thornton do not explicitly present them on a continuum like Figure 7.1, we see potential in doing so as Figure 7.2 illustrates. We're not suggesting each category has an equal opposite. Instead, any combination from left or right will lead to directive or facilitative interventions respectively. Whereas a combination from both sides will place you somewhere in the middle.

When you reflect on your interaction, you will likely discover that you use a combination of interventions and fall at various points on the continuum, depending on your mentees, your personal style, and the situation. Although the ultimate goal of mentoring is learner ownership supported by the facilitative end, your mentees, for a number of reasons, will begin at various points along the path. Your interactions likely reflect their starting points.

You may also feel a need to add an intervention category. Heron himself invites you to test out his framework in practice and modify it. He says, "There is nothing sacred or unchallengeable about the number 'six,' nor about the way the whole thing is conceptually put together."[12] Our mentors have found some benefit in doing as he suggests and have proposed other interventions. Some have described an illuminating category, for example, whereby a mentor shines light on a problem so that a mentee can figure it out autonomously. Others, concerned with *affect* and *values* issues, have chosen the word *refining* to describe a gradual (and largely collaborative) process of filtering out negative attitudes toward teaching or students.

In "Now It's Your Turn," you'll have an opportunity to reflect on, test out, and modify interventions. First, though, let's consider two perspectives from which to choose points on the continuum.

MEETING NEEDS AND REACHING GOALS THROUGH FEEDBACK

Decisions about where you fall on the continuum are in part made based on the needs of your mentees and the goals you're working toward.

HERE'S WHAT HAPPENED: SELF-ASSESSING MENTORING STYLES

In their mentoring course, a group of mentors were asked to assess their personal mentoring style. In part, they considered Heron's intervention framework. Their comments on using different categories are listed below.

Prescriptive
- *The new teachers had no experience or skills from which to pull ideas for how to decrease their talk time.*

Informative
- *Include helpful information (regarding culture or theory that may influence the success of a lesson)*
- *There was need for a complete change of mindset in the teachers.*

Confronting
- *Calling her attention to her half-hearted monitoring . . . encouraged her that as the teacher, it is acceptable to interrupt them as they work and ask them to explain to her what they have discussed*
- *With continual reassurance that she "is the teacher" and that the students respect her in that role and therefore will accept, and even expect, her to hold them accountable to the assigned tasks.*

Cathartic
- *A time of emotional release for the teachers*
- *Because of her personality, direct confrontation would have led to a heightened defensiveness . . . allowed her to share her heart . . .*

- *Picked up on her feelings of helplessness and discouragement through previous conversations*
- *Make room for the discovery and action that still needed to take place.*

Catalytic
- *Questions that will cause the teachers to think about previous conversations or coursework done during their training and assess portions of their plan accordingly*
- *To reflect upon the pacing of his lesson . . . would the students actually be able to retain the new information they had learned? . . . By questioning [the teacher was] encouraged toward self-discovery.*

Supportive
- *Simply celebrate growth and success in creating activities that are well thought out and reflect the stated course goals*
- *To build and encourage morale*
- *Due to her personality style*
- *Allowed me to be more prescriptive in the end.*

WHAT DO YOU THINK?

1. How well do the mentors' understandings of intervention categories match yours?
2. As you've thought about where you fall on the directive-facilitative continuum and which intervention categories you might use, how does your reasoning fit with that of these mentors?
3. What are other reasons why you would use (or not use) a particular style?

Drawing on the experiences of these mentors, some of the reasons why you may choose (or not choose) a particular style are listed below.

Needs/Goals

Your choice of intervention categories may be related to the *knowledge* and *skills* needs of your mentees. You may directly tell them about a principle or theory that they have not yet been exposed to (like teacher talk time or an aspect of the learners' culture). You may choose to ask a catalytic question that reminds them of "previous conversations" or one of your essential questions. An intervention style may also be chosen as a means of making progress toward *affect* and *values* benchmarks. An attitude ("half-hearted") might tie into a teaching skill (monitoring group work). This is where some of our mentors have applied a refining category as they and their mentees collaboratively make progress toward a mutually agreed upon value.

Also at play here are the needs of the learners. A confronting approach (about monitoring group work, for example) may come across as less directive when the focus is on the expectations or feelings of the learners, especially when those observations also benefit the teacher. Moreover, a mentee may find it easier to self-evaluate when asked to view an issue (like pacing) from the students' perspective.

Affective Filter

An intervention style may also be selected as a means of lowering the affective filter. You may choose a cathartic approach, for example, as an "emotional release" when mentees are facing professional or even life challenges. A supportive approach might work when they're feeling anxiety over being observed (or some other aspect of the mentoring relationship), and you want to "celebrate growth" or "build and encourage morale." Either a more facilitative or directive approach may be chosen because of a mentee's personality and preferences. Moreover, one may be selected in order to "make room" affectively for another.

Balancing Input and Output

With the ultimate goal of mentoring in mind, most of our mentors in training have attempted to work toward catalytic interventions.[13] When they have chosen other types, often they were making room for "the discovery and action that still needed to take place." Moreover, they have looked for ways to increase mentee output by asking questions that in the end would "cause the teachers to think . . . and assess . . . accordingly," and facilitate "self-discovery."

PRAGMATICS FOR FEEDBACK

Another perspective from which to choose where you fall between directive and facilitative feedback is a sociocultural one. In particular, it is important to consider your intended message and how to get it across in ways that are polite, appropriate, and palatable. Wajnryb[14] and Bailey[15] have discussed in some detail the sociocultural aspects of mentoring interactions and the mitigation of negative feedback. The challenge, they explain, is mitigating enough to avoid affective issues while still getting your message across.

Feedback of any sort can be softened with word choice, sentence structure, non-verbal cues like tone or facial expression, or emoticons. Facilitative feedback is by nature mitigated. It is frequently given indirectly and often in question form so as to engage mentees in dialog and elicit self-evaluation. Consider a situation like the one in "What Do You Think?" below.

WHAT DO YOU THINK?

After an observation, a mentor wants to talk with a teacher about his/her grammar explanation. Some potential conversation openers are in Table 7.1. Order them from unmitigated to mitigated, direct to indirect, and directive to facilitative? Which one best communicates the intended message without being hurtful or putting mentees on the defensive? Which opener would you choose?

Table 7.1 **Conversation Openers**

What are some different ways you've used to help students figure out a grammar structure?	Let's talk through your lesson and you tell me what you liked and didn't like.
Let's talk about what students might have understood and how you judged that.	The students seemed a little confused by your grammar explanation.
Which objectives did the students reach, and which did they struggle most with?	Your grammar explanation was confusing.
The students seemed a little confused by your grammar explanation (said with a smile and gentle tone).	

When considering which opener to choose, your answer may have been, "It depends." In many ways, how you interact is determined by your mentees, the situation, and more. In order to figure out how to communicate with teachers in appropriate ways, we have negotiated our own pragmatics for feedback with our mentors in training. Some of

PRAGMATICS FOR FEEDBACK		
Directive ←		**Facilitative** →
Allows for less mitigation		**Requires more mitigation**
Genuine, collaborative relationship You have authority/power/status	Relationship	Distant relationship You have no authority/power/status
Public/impersonal information Positive effect on listener	Message	Private/personal information Negative effect on listener
Teacher feels successful Issues are easy to fix Issues are common sense	Situation	Teacher feels like a failure Issues are complicated Issues leave room for opinion

Figure 7.3 Pragmatics for Feedback

our ideas are summarized in Figure 7.3. They are drawn from politeness factors English language learners may need to consider when developing socio-cultural competence.[16] We've tweaked them to reflect communication that may occur between a mentor and mentee, from the mentor's perspective. They are represented on a scale, which means a mentor's feedback could fall somewhere in the middle. While you consider our ideas, reflect on the questions below.

WHAT DO YOU THINK?

1. These ideas are based on politeness factors for North American English because most of our mentors have come from that part of the world. How might the scale differ if you and/or your mentees are from another part of the world?
2. How might the scale differ for each of your mentees based on personal and cultural factors?

On the left side of the scale, are settings that allow for (but do not require) less mitigation and more directive feedback. On the right are settings that require more mitigation and where a facilitative style may be most appropriate. Each of the three factors, relationship, message, and situation, are described in more detail below. Remember that our scale is based on politeness rules for North American English. In "Now It's Your Turn," you'll have a chance to consider how to adapt the scale to other settings, including making allowances for personal differences.

Relationship

Throughout this book, we have assumed that mentoring occurs in the context of a genuine and collaborative relationship. Our scale, then, illustrates potential challenges when no such relationship has been established. If you're a stranger coming in from the outside or meeting online rather than face-to-face, building rapport first will make communication easier and allow for a wider range.

Complicating factors include whether you've been assigned to mentor or if it is a voluntary setting. We recommend leaning toward the facilitative end. However, in the first setting, you may be given the *right* to be more directive. The second may require some facilitative finesse until you earn a certain level of respect from your mentees. A previously established relationship outside the mentoring context can further muddle the situation. How do you decide where to fall on the continuum then?

Message

In most North American settings, praise will usually have a positive effect on your mentees and can appropriately be said directly and in a public venue. (Note that there are personal differences. Some people, for instance, automatically reject a compliment because they always view themselves negatively.) Anything interpreted as a criticism, however, is likely to have a negative effect. It is personal, should be private, and may be best communicated in a facilitative way. (Again, take into account personal differences.) Negative feedback itself, though, may flow from personal to impersonal. For example, talking about a mentee's clothing is more personal than mentioning their whiteboard use. A complaint about the situation, a lack of equipment in the classroom, for instance, is even more impersonal and allows for more directive feedback.

Situation

Although again there are personal differences, when your mentees feel successful, they may have more emotional energy to receive directive feedback. When they feel as if they've failed, however, they may first need some care and concern (with a supportive or cathartic intervention). Then, out of a desire to fix what went wrong, they may be more open to self-evaluation on the facilitative end.

A mentor once ended her conversation with a teacher this way, "Oh, and don't chew gum in class." The issue was common sense, and the teacher knew that. You may find yourself repeating certain statements to your mentees like, "Use a larger font in your multimedia presentations so that students in the back can see." Issues like these are common sense and easily remedied, and so they are also easy to approach directly. However, facilitative approaches may work better when issues are complicated and leave room for opinion. In fact, some of our mentors have found, with more complex issues, that they change their minds after allowing mentees to self-evaluate. After an observation when Sandra asked her mentee why she called on students primarily from the left side of the room, the teacher responded, "I alternate which side of the classroom I teach from because I know I often choose students on that side. Today was the left side."

FEEDBACK FOR FACILITATIVE MENTORING

More than once in this chapter, we've said or at least implied, "It depends." Where you fall on the feedback continuum is determined by your mentees and their settings. We've also said that the goal is to lean toward the facilitative end. You could gradually progress toward that end in a series of interactions with a mentee. At other times, you may want to start there and then work backward until your mentee figures out the problem you're bringing to her/his awareness. The next chapter will give you some ideas about how to navigate the continuum with specific questioning techniques. First, however, it's your turn to make some decisions about your feedback modes and styles.

NOW IT'S YOUR TURN

Task 7.1 is designed to be done with your current or future mentees. Then, you can write about it in your mentoring journal or report to your mentor support group. With Tasks 7.2 and 7.3, you have some options. You could complete them alone and use them as a journal topic. Or you could collaborate with your mentor support group. Task 7.3 could potentially be done with a mentee.

Task 7.1: Interaction Analysis

Analyze how to interact with mentees:

1. Interview (face-to-face or using an online platform) 3–5 current or future mentees about modes of communication and types of feedback mentors

Table 7.2 **Interaction Analysis**

	Mentee 1:	Mentee 2:	Mentee 3:
Modes of communication			
Directive-facilitative			
Intervention categories			
Interaction analysis			

have used when giving them advice. You can use (or adapt) Table 7.2 to record what you find. Some potential questions are listed below.

- When a mentor has given you feedback _____ (on a lesson plan, after an observation, on your teaching as a whole), was it given orally or in written form, face-to-face or through email or some other online platform?
- What were the benefits and drawbacks of the different methods of communication?
- If you were giving advice to a mentor about how to communicate with a teacher _____ (orally or in writing, face-to-face or virtually, etc.), what would you say?
- How have mentors given you advice? (You could give them choices: directly or indirectly, making statements or asking questions, etc. You could also show them the Intervention Framework and allow them to choose categories.)
- Which types of feedback do you prefer?
- If you were giving advice to a mentor about how to communicate with a teacher, what types of feedback would you recommend?

2. After the interviews, analyze how to interact with each teacher. If you were giving them feedback: (a) Which modes of communication would work best? (b) Where would your interactions fall on the directive-facilitative continuum? (c) Which combination of Heron's intervention categories might work best?
3. If you are currently mentoring, try out one of your individualized approaches with a mentee.

4. In your mentoring journal or with your mentor support group, summarize what you've learned and any trends you see. Make suggestions to mentors (or yourself) about how to communicate with mentees.

Task 7.2: Interaction Framework

After completing Task 7.1, do some further analysis about what works and doesn't and what trends you see. As mentioned above, Heron invites readers to add to his six categories. What category would you add based on your mentees' needs? Design your own intervention framework, or create your own model of feedback.

Task 7.3: Pragmatics for Feedback

As mentioned above, the scale in Figure 7.3 is based on North American English. If you and/or your mentees are from another part of the world, how would the scale differ? How would it differ based not only on **cultural** factors but also **personal**? Design your own Pragmatics for Feedback. If necessary, draw on the knowledge and experiences of your (potential) mentees or others in the local culture.

NOTES

1. Angi Malderez, "Mentoring," in *The Cambridge Guide to Second Language Teacher Education*, ed. Anne Burns and Jack C. Richards (Cambridge: Cambridge University Press, 2009), Kindle edition.
2. Melissa K. Smith and Marilyn Lewis, "The Language Teaching Practicum: Perspectives from Mentors," *The Teacher Trainer* 23, no. 2 (2009), 5–8.
3. For more on the versatility of WeChat and its capabilities, see https://nyti.ms/2b4n4ew or www.economist.com/news/business/21703428-chinas-wechat-shows-way-social-medias-future-wechats-world.
4. A Virtual Private Network (VPN) provides access to the internet through an encrypted connection, which both keeps data secure and allows access to sites that are blocked in a country like China.
5. Malderez, *The Cambridge Guide*, 267.
6. Ewen Arnold, "Assessing the Quality of Mentoring: Sinking or Learning to Swim," *ELT Journal* 60, no. 2 (2006): 119, https:/doi.org/10.1093/elt/cci098.
7. Mick Randall and Barbara Thornton, *Advising and Supporting Teachers* (Cambridge: Cambridge University Press, 2001), 79.
8. Ibid., 80.
9. Christopher Stillwell, "The Collaborative Development of Teacher Training Skills," *ELT Journal* 63, no. 4 (2009): 357–358, https:/doi.org/10.1093/elt/ccn068.
10. John Heron, *Helping the Client: A Creative Practical Guide*, 5th ed. (London: Sage Publications, 2001), Kindle edition, chap. 1.

11. Randall and Thornton, *Advising and Supporting Teachers*.
12. Ibid., chap. 1.
13. Melissa K. Smith and Marilyn Lewis, "Toward Facilitative Mentoring and Catalytic Interventions," *ELT Journal* 69, no. 2 (2015), 140–150, https:/doi.org/10.1093/elt/ccu075.
14. Ruth Wajnryb, "The Pragmatics of Feedback: A Study of Mitigation in the Supervisory Discourse of TESOL Teacher Educators" (PhD diss., Macquarie University, 1994), http://hdl.handle.net/1959.14/23100.
15. Kathleen M. Bailey, *Language Teacher Supervision* (Cambridge: Cambridge University Press, 2006), https:/doi.org/10.1017/CBO9780511667329.
16. Tasha Bleistein, Melissa K. Smith, and Marilyn Lewis, *Teaching Speaking* (Alexandria, VA: TESOL International Association, 2013).

REFERENCES

Arnold, Ewen. "Assessing the Quality of Mentoring: Sinking or Learning to Swim." *ELT Journal* 60, no. 2 (2006): 117–124. https:/doi.org/10.1093/elt/cci098.
Bailey, Kathleen M. *Language Teacher Supervision*. Cambridge: Cambridge University Press, 2006. https:/doi.org/10.1017/CBO9780511667329.
Bleistein, Tasha, Melissa K. Smith, and Marilyn Lewis. *Teaching Speaking*. Alexandria, VA: TESOL International Association, 2013.
Heron, John. *Helping the Client: A Creative Practical Guide*. 5th ed. London: Sage Publications, 2001. Kindle edition.
Malderez, Angi. "Mentoring." In *The Cambridge Guide to Second Language Teacher Education*, edited by Anne Burns and Jack C. Richards, Chapter 26. Cambridge: Cambridge University Press, 2009. Kindle edition.
Randall, Mick and Barbara Thornton. *Advising and Supporting Teachers*. Cambridge: Cambridge University Press, 2001.
Smith, Melissa K. and Marilyn Lewis. "The Language Teaching Practicum: Perspectives from Mentors." *The Teacher Trainer* 23, no. 2 (2009): 5–8.
Smith, Melissa K. and Marilyn Lewis. "Toward Facilitative Mentoring and Catalytic Interventions." *ELT Journal* 69, no. 2 (2015): 140–150. https:/doi.org/10.1093/elt/ccu075.
Stillwell, Christopher. "The Collaborative Development of Teacher Training Skills." *ELT Journal* 63, no. 4 (2009): 353–362. https:/doi.org/10.1093/elt/ccn068.
Wajnryb, Ruth. "The Pragmatics of Feedback: A Study of Mitigation in the Supervisory Discourse of TESOL Teacher Educators." PhD diss., Macquarie University, 1994. http://hdl.handle.net/1959.14/23100.

CHAPTER 8

The Mentor as Questioner

WHAT DO YOU THINK?

1. Why is asking questions an important part of mentoring interactions?
2. Are some types of questions more helpful than others?
3. Are some ways of asking more helpful than others?
4. How do our intentions play a role in how our questions come across?
5. When mentees get stuck, how do questions help them move forward?

Speech acts have been described as the "basic or minimal units of linguistic communication."[1] They could also be described as the basic units of mentoring interactions. Having just reflected on a mentor's traditional feedback role, the first speech acts that come to mind are giving advice and making suggestions. However, mentors engage in many more speech acts: discussing, agreeing, disagreeing, complimenting or praising, talking about the past, stating future intentions, and dealing with emotions, among others. Questions are what characterize the speech acts of mentors. Whether sharing opinions or feelings or talking about the past or future, mentors, particularly ones who are attempting to facilitate interactions, are asking for information and input from their mentees as much as or more than giving it.

The last two chapters have shown how guiding teachers through the Zone of Proximal Development (ZPD) usually happens through interactions. These often take the form of feedback conversations that can occur face-to-face or virtually. You've also reflected on pragmatics for feedback and how to communicate with your mentees in appropriate and palatable ways. What's left is the content of those conversations and specifically questions. As the opening illustration in Chapter 6 showed, asking questions requires some finesse. This chapter, then, will offer ideas for refining your questioning skills.

You will notice that we ask more questions than usual throughout this chapter. That is intentional. It will give you a sense of how it feels to be questioned and how different types of questions work. Also, we hope that you will be encouraged to figure out some of the answers in negotiation with your mentees within their classroom contexts.

THE IMPORTANCE OF QUESTIONS

For a number of reasons, questions are an important part of interactive mentoring. They play a role in raising mentees' awareness of areas that need attention.[2] They take reflection and collaboration to a place where mentors and mentees become "co-inquirers into problems."[3] Moreover, they help teachers peel back the onion and reflect on how the inner layers of professional, personal, and spiritual identity, including a teacher's "mission" or "calling," inspire the outer layers of what s/he does in the classroom.[4] Furthermore, they support mentee ownership. They're part of the "catalytic toolkit" whereby mentors facilitate autonomy.[5] Although the co-inquiring mentor may contribute to the answers, questions stimulate mentees to notice, reflect, respond, and then take responsibility for conclusions.

TYPES OF QUESTIONS

Questions are an important part of the mentoring process; however, not just any question will do. You've likely had experiences in mentoring (and life) where a question you asked was either answered in a completely unexpected way or had a surprising result. "If only I were better at asking questions" is a common lament we've heard from our mentors and have made ourselves. One way of approaching this challenge is to consider the types of questions you ask. The results of conversational analysis and studies of teachers' classroom language all have suggestions, ranging from being sure to ask a mixture of question types to looking at differences between the speaker's intention and the receiver's understanding. Let's examine these two perspectives.

Variety

One of the many uses of Bloom's Taxonomy has been to help teachers ask questions that prompt thinking beyond the basic recall level. For mentors, it is another device to add to their catalytic toolkit. In Chapter 6, we presented Bloom's Taxonomy for Mentoring as a tool for understanding interactions. It can also be used as a device for asking a variety of questions that encourage mentees to reflect more deeply (as you take them down the taxonomy). Figure 8.1 offers a sample of what questions might look like before or after a lesson observation. They flow from surface to deep.

In language teaching, a common distinction is made between display and referential questions. Display questions ask for information already known, referential for information not known. Display questions are often used as a way to manage the classroom, check for comprehension, or elicit certain patterns from students. They may have a place as long as they aren't "silly" because they are overly obvious.[6] Referential questions, on the other hand, may be preferred because they are or at least imitate authentic communication. Looking at the questions in Figure 8.1, are they display or referential? Do both types seem to play a role in mentoring? How?

Remembering: *Last week we discussed ___. Which of those ideas has stayed in your mind as worth trying out?*

Understanding: *What do you know about the students in that class and how they might respond to that idea?*

Applying: *What happened when you did try it out?*

Analyzing: *Thinking of what you tried today, how would you describe: a) the students' participation, b) the suitability of the resources you prepared, and c) the timing?*

Evaluating: *Overall how would you asses the value of this idea in your class with your students?*

Creating: *Based on what happened in the classroom, your analysis and evaluation today, and how that fits with what you learned in your initial teacher training, how would you devise your own version of the idea for use in a future class?*

Values: *How could you use an idea like the one you tried to encourage respect for individuals or cultures (or another agreed upon value)?*

Figure 8.1 Bloom's Taxonomy for Mentoring: Questions

Another common distinction made for both language teachers and mentors is open versus closed questions. Randall and Thornton point out that what makes a question open or closed has more to do with its purpose than its type. They use the example, "What do you feel about the use of games in lessons?"[7] If eliciting how a teacher feels, it's open-ended. If asking for theories or principles, it's closed (perhaps in a setting where the mentor usually engages in one-way transmission instead of collaborative dialog). What seem to be the purposes for the questions in Figure 8.1? Are they open or closed? Do both types play a role in mentoring interactions?

Intentions

Randall and Thornton's discussion about open versus closed questions illustrates an important point. Whatever the question type, what counts in your mentoring interactions is how it comes across. In part, this is determined by your intentions. As in Randall and Thornton's example, are you eliciting feelings or theories? Are you intending for your mentees to display what you (and they) already know, or are you attempting to engage in authentic discussion? Do you want them to see your perspective or come to their own conclusions? Going back to Chapter 7, how does the intent of your questions come across differently in face-to-face versus virtual settings?

In order to understand intentions, let's return to the directive-facilitative continuum set up in the last chapter. It would be natural to suppose that directive feedback takes the shape of statements, facilitative as questions. However, feedback in the form of a question can range from directive to facilitative. In fact, formulating (grammatically) directive feedback as a question is one way to mitigate it (or using intonation to make a statement sound like a question). Consider the questions in "What Do You Think?"

WHAT DO YOU THINK?

Analyze the questions in Table 8.1 and consider what types they are: (1) What level are they on Bloom's Taxonomy for Mentoring? (2) Are they display or referential? (3) Are they open or closed? (4) Do they seem directive or facilitative?

As you considered whether the questions are directive or facilitative, you may have returned to our answer from the last chapter: "It depends."

Table 8.1 **Question Analysis**

Question	Bloom's Taxonomy	Display or Referential	Open or Closed	Directive or Facilitative
Do you think the students felt they had enough opportunity to practice the language taught?				
The students really seemed to enjoy the practice activity. I wondered if they were trying hard to please you because there was an observer in the room. How do they generally respond to practice activities?				
I kept track of teacher input and student output while I was observing. Would you like to make a guess as to the ratio?				
I kept track of teacher input and student output while I was observing. Here you can see the ratio. What do you think about it?				
How do you think the students felt about the practice activity?				
What should the balance look like between input and output in the language classroom?				
What are some steps you will take in your next class to reach the input-output ratio you think is appropriate?				
Who should be on stage in your classroom, you or your students?				

How a message is received is determined in part by what you intend. It is also influenced by the situation and your relationship with your mentees. In order to illustrate further, let's return to the example at the beginning of Chapter 6. When her employee interpreted her questions as suggestions, the employer wondered if her communication skills and in particular her questions needed work. She also considered other possibilities:

1. The employer is the age of the employee's mother. Did the employee assume she was being given advice like her mother offers?
2. The employee is Chinese and the employer American. They have a more equal relationship than in similar settings in Chinese society.

Still, in a place where power distance is high, did the employee assume she was receiving advice from someone who has the right to offer it?
3. Because the employee started the conversation and seemed open, was she looking for advice in whatever the employer said?
4. Did the employee and employer's shared system of values make it easier for them to come to the same conclusions?

There are no fixed rules for questions in mentoring interactions, and there is no secret formula. Instead, what might be most valuable is to question your questions.

1. What is the message you intend? (In part, do you intend to be directive or facilitative?)
2. How does your message come across to your mentee?
3. How does your relationship and/or the situation play a role in how it comes across?
4. How are these factors complicated given personal and cultural differences?
5. How is expressing intent different in face-to-face versus virtual interactions?

QUESTIONING TECHNIQUES

In working with our mentors in training, we've noticed that some have developed personal questioning techniques. We've written about this in another place,[8] but will summarize four of their techniques below and give examples.

Sandra's Scaffold

This questioning technique starts with information mentees have already learned, possibly something the mentor offered them in a directive manner or an informative intervention. The mentor then draws the mentee toward the facilitative end by asking questions within the framework of the previously learned information. The questions in Figure 8.1 are an example of how Sandra's Scaffold Technique might work. Within the framework of a previously discussed idea, the mentor can ask questions that facilitate reflection and self-evaluation, both working down Bloom's Taxonomy for Mentoring and toward ownership.

Cheryl's Funnel

In an attempt to engage in facilitative mentoring, the mentor tries to draw mentees toward a conclusion through a series of questions that start broad and become narrower. The conversation may begin with an event in the lesson and distill into one aspect of classroom management or a teaching principle/skill. The series of questions may also take mentees through the process of noticing, reflecting, responding, and taking ownership. In some ways, the mentor is working backward from facilitative to directive, first offering an opportunity for autonomy and then gradually reversing to a point mentees are ready for. In "Here's What Happened: Funnel Technique," Cheryl's interaction with her mentees illustrates how her technique works.

HERE'S WHAT HAPPENED: FUNNEL TECHNIQUE

After observing a group of mentees team-teach, Cheryl led them toward conclusions about the use of group work. A condensed version of her interaction is below.

Cheryl	How did it feel to choose the groups in that moment?
T1	(Explains he felt good about how he divided groups.)
Cheryl	*Could you have chosen before you got to class?*
T1	(Indicates understanding.)
Cheryl	*What's the benefit?*
T1	(Sees what she's getting at and agrees.)
Cheryl	(Returns to a point in the lesson when a group didn't have an answer.) *What do you do?*
T1	(Has some ideas about what he could do differently and how he could help them.)
Cheryl	*What else?*
T1	*Encourage them.*
Cheryl	(Seems to want to go farther about how to manage/prevent such a situation and so repeats question.)
T2	*Give a hint.*
Cheryl	*When?*
T2	*When they are giving the answer.*
Cheryl	*When students are working in groups, what is the teacher doing?*
T1	*Monitor.*
Cheryl	*How?*

T1	*See what they are doing.*
Cheryl	(Continues asking questions to explore monitoring more closely. Questions them about what they could do and gives examples from her own teaching.)

Norm's Springboard

This technique gives voice to a pattern many of our mentors have used in their mentoring interactions. It may also be the most facilitative of the four techniques presented here. The mentor begins with a broad question intending to use it as a springboard to peel back the layers and explore deeper issues. Although the mentor is available as a co-inquirer, the purpose of this technique is to facilitate reflection, self-evaluation, and ownership. Adaptations of Norm's Springboard questions are included below.

1. How do/did you feel about the lesson/today's class/your teaching?
2. Does anything stand out to you as a strength in your lesson/today's class/your teaching?
3. What stands out to you as something you could improve on or might like to change in the future?
4. Do you have any questions about ___?
5. Is there anything I could help you with for ___?

Rachel's Defend Their Honor

Coming from a different perspective, this technique is more overtly focused on affective issues than the other three. When Rachel first noted her use of this technique, she was looking for a way to encourage critical self-reflection without coming across as pejorative. Instead, in order to build trust, the mentor asks an evaluation question, in a way that indicates support rather than opposition (perhaps through manner or tone), and then s/he listens while the mentee "defends" her/his decision. The defense may persuade the mentor, or the mentee's self-evaluation may raise awareness and lead her/him to take responsibility for a needed change. Some possible question prompts are listed below.

1. How effective do you think ___ was/is?
2. How well did/does ___ work?
3. Why did you ___?

___ Technique

We promised four techniques. This fifth one is yours. Although you can employ the techniques above and even customize them to fit your own style and situations, you may also want to design a personal technique as another device for your toolbox.

QUESTIONING FOR REFLECTION AND AUTONOMY

When you think about your current or future mentees or other teachers you know, can you identify ones who are enthusiastically working toward growth? Do others seem unable to move forward? Why? The difference between the two groups may be their mindsets.[9] The second group may be struggling with fixed mindsets that are blocking their progress. Fixed mindsets are ways of thinking rooted in the belief that people's intelligence and skills are unchangeable no matter their effort. In contrast, the first group's growth mindset encourages them to develop through hard work.

Your mentees may need to explore when and how their fixed mindsets interfere with growth. Awareness and reflection are important steps toward progress. However, your questions also play a role as Table 8.2 illustrates.

Table 8.2 **Fixed vs. Growth Mindsets in Mentoring Interactions**

A Fixed Mindset . . .	A Growth Mindset . . .
Focuses on whether what a teacher did (in a lesson or class) was right or wrong	Encourages reflection and self-evaluation: • How did you decide to ___ (as you were planning/teaching)? • What problems did you have? How did you solve them? • What's something new you've learned? • What's something you still need to learn?
Gives a teacher the *right* answer	Encourages learner ownership: • What's your next step? • What do you need to do in order to figure it out?
Praises a teacher for intelligence or talent	Focuses on the mentee's effort and growth: • What was easy? What was difficult? Why? • What are you going to do differently next time?

INTERACTIVE MENTORING

In using questions in feedback conversations and other mentoring interactions, the overall goal is to lead toward reflection and mentee ownership. As we've implied before, this process is a journey. When it becomes wearisome or mentees face a roadblock, an apt question may be just what's needed to remove the barriers, smooth the path, and encourage forward movement.

NOW IT'S YOUR TURN

All of the tasks below include elements that assume you are currently mentoring. Feel free to adapt them. For example, after making your list of question prompts in Task 8.1, try them out with someone from your mentor support group (virtually if necessary), or when completing Task 8.3, consider what you've heard colleagues say.

Task 8.1: Question Prompts

Bertie, many years after participating in our mentor training, gave advice to us in response to our lament, "If only I were better at asking questions." She suggested making a list of question prompts to guide interactions with mentees. What prompts would you include? Below, we've listed twenty prompts that came up in this chapter. Try personalizing the list before your next mentoring encounter. (How would you order or group the prompts for ease of use, for example? Would you add, combine, or leave any out?) After trying it out, revise it for subsequent interactions.

1. Which of those ideas has stayed in your mind . . . ?
2. What do you know about . . . ?
3. What happened when you . . . ?
4. How would you describe . . . ?
5. How would you assess . . . ?
6. How would you devise . . . ?
7. How could you encourage . . . ?
8. How do students usually respond to . . . ?
9. Would you like to make a guess at . . . ?
10. What do you think about . . . ?
11. How do you think the students felt about . . . ?
12. What should ___ look like . . . ?
13. What are some steps you will take to . . . ?
14. How did it feel to . . . ?

15. Could you have . . . ?
16. When students are ___, what is the teacher doing?
17. When the teacher is ___, what are the students doing?
18. How effective is . . . ?
19. How well did ___ work . . . ?
20. Why did you . . . ?

Task 8.2: ___ Technique

Record a mentoring interaction or look at a written record. (You could use data from Task 6.2.) Alternatively, journal about an interaction. Analyze your questioning patterns (or the patterns of the mentor in the interaction):

1. What questioning techniques do you notice?
2. Do the techniques fit with ones described in this chapter, or do you have your own? (Or does the mentor in the interaction have her/his own?)
3. What would you call the personal questioning technique? How would you describe it?

Write in your mentoring journal about the technique, or share it with your mentor support group.

Task 8.3: Encouraging a Growth Mindset

If you are currently mentoring, think about some of the things you hear your mentees say or imply (about their knowledge/skill, progress, or what happens in class) that indicates a fixed mindset. Brainstorm for questions you could ask that would encourage a growth mindset. We started Table 8.3 for you.

Table 8.3 Encouraging a Growth Mindset

WHAT MENTEES MIGHT SAY:	MENTOR RESPONSE:
(Fixed Mindset)	(Growth Mindset)
I'm not good at this.	What could you do to figure it out?
The students never bring their textbooks to class.	What steps could you take to encourage them to bring their textbooks with them each time?

(Continued)

Table 8.3 **Continued**

WHAT MENTEES MIGHT SAY: (Fixed Mindset)	MENTOR RESPONSE: (Growth Mindset)
The activity went well.	What's something you learned from planning and implementing it?

NOTES

1. John R. Searle, *Speech Acts: An Essay in the Philosophy of Language* (Cambridge: Cambridge University Press, 1969), Kindle edition, chap. 1.
2. Kathleen M. Bailey, *Language Teacher Supervision* (Cambridge: Cambridge University Press, 2006), https:/doi.org/10.1017/CBO9780511667329.
3. Steve Mann and Elaine Hau Hing Tang, "The Role of Mentoring in Supporting Novice English Language Teachers in Hong Kong," *TESOL Quarterly* 46, no. 3 (2012): 484, https:/doi.org/10.1002/tesq.38.
4. Fred Korthagen and Angelo Vasalos, "Levels in Reflection: Core Reflection as a Means to Enhance Professional Growth," *Teachers and Teaching: Theory and Practice* 11, no. 1 (2005): 53, https:/doi.org/10.1080/1354060042000337093.
5. Mick Randall and Barbara Thornton, *Advising and Supporting Teachers* (Cambridge: Cambridge University Press, 2001), 124.
6. H. Douglas Brown and Heekyeong Lee, *Teaching by Principles*, 4th ed. (White Plains, NY: Pearson Education, 2015), 264.
7. Randall and Thornton, *Advising and Supporting Teachers*, 125.

8. Melissa K. Smith and Marilyn Lewis, "Toward Facilitative Mentoring and Catalytic Interventions," *ELT Journal* 69, no. 2 (2015), 140–150, https:/doi.org/10.1093/elt/ccu075.
9. Carol S. Dweck, *Mindset: The New Psychology of Success* (New York: Ballantine Books, 2016), Kindle edition.

REFERENCES

Bailey, Kathleen M. *Language Teacher Supervision*. Cambridge: Cambridge University Press, 2006. https:/doi.org/10.1017/CBO9780511667329.
Brown, H. Douglas and Heekyeong Lee. *Teaching by Principles*. 4th ed. White Plains, NY: Pearson Education, 2015.
Dweck, Carol S. *Mindset: The New Psychology of Success*. New York: Ballantine Books, 2016. Kindle edition.
Korthagen, Fred and Angelo Vasalos. "Levels in Reflection: Core Reflection as a Means to Enhance Professional Growth." *Teachers and Teaching: Theory and Practice* 11, no. 1 (2005): 47–71. https:/doi.org/10.1080/1354060042000337093.
Mann, Steve and Elaine Hau Hing Tang. "The Role of Mentoring in Supporting Novice English Language Teachers in Hong Kong." *TESOL Quarterly* 46, no. 3 (2012): 472–495. https:/doi.org/10.1002/tesq.38.
Randall, Mick and Barbara Thornton. *Advising and Supporting Teachers*. Cambridge: Cambridge University Press, 2001.
Searle, John R. *Speech Acts: An Essay in the Philosophy of Language*. Cambridge: Cambridge University Press, 1969. Kindle edition.
Smith, Melissa K. and Marilyn Lewis. "Toward Facilitative Mentoring and Catalytic Interventions." *ELT Journal* 69, no. 2 (2015): 140–150. https:/doi.org/10.1093/elt/ccu075.

SECTION IV

Task-Based Mentoring

Maybe the next time you observe, it would be a good idea to have something beforehand that you have talked to her about, either something that she wants you to observe about her teaching or even something that you want to observe in her teaching that you are having a problem with. [She] is a great teacher and I know you can learn a lot from her.

—Carlos (giving feedback to himself)

There was one teacher who came to me later asking for advice and help in creating and using portfolios. That was rewarding, and I felt like my efforts had been useful for at least one teacher. I was also able to see how impractical some of my advice had been in the session. If I were to do this session again, I would have done it differently and included more samples rather than theoretical ideas.

—Rachel

I loved doing that project. It has been a pivotal part of my experience in fact. I am so thankful that those teachers were willing to participate so wholeheartedly for me—and for them.

—Rachel

CHAPTER 9

Classroom Observation

WHAT DO YOU THINK?

1. What can we learn from teachers' experiences being observed and mentors' experiences as observers?
2. What issues may a mentor face when observing a mentee?
3. What are some ways to manage these issues?
4. What are some considerations when planning for and implementing an observation?

Mentoring tasks are authentic and collaborative (between mentor and mentee) learning activities that should lead toward more success in the mentee's classroom. Task-based mentoring is the process of using these activities to encourage teacher learning, reflection, and ownership. The next chapter talks about group mentoring tasks, and then Chapter 11 introduces action research as a collaborative activity for learning teaching. First, though, let's begin with what is often seen as the primary task of a mentoring relationship: classroom observation.

Three veteran English language teachers in different settings were asked to reflect on being observed. One shared her positive experiences. The other two noted the same benefit: an outside, objective view of their classrooms. In her musings, however, the third teacher, first listed her negative experiences as if needing to clear out a path to the positives. Dovetailing with feedback, observation is often seen as a mentor's primary role. Because it may also be the main source of affective issues, we start with these negatives, hoping to clear out a path to the positives.

IN THEIR OWN WORDS: TEACHERS REFLECT ON BEING OBSERVED

One Teacher's List of Negatives

1. Observations with high stakes (potential effects on job retention or promotion, for example)
2. When observers haven't told me what things they are hoping to see or why they're coming
3. When I know I can't and shouldn't actually produce the high-quality/activity-packed/technology-packed pull-out-all-the-stops kind of lesson . . . AND, then, when I feel pressure to pull out all the stops
4. When there's an observer effect on my students
5. When observations make me nervous and I can't just be myself
6. When observers seem to miss the big picture and focus on what seems minor
7. When observers leave without saying a word of commendation . . . or without saying anything at all
8. When observers (who are also colleagues) don't welcome me to observe their classes.

A Second Teacher's Path to the Positives

I was nervous about observations when I first started teaching but now they don't bother me. But, maybe that's because I feel mostly comfortable at my current school? Perhaps at another school it would be scary. Or maybe it's because I have never lost a job due to a negative observation? Or because people have always been friendly, even if there is advice that they need to give me? No one has ever been overly critical.

WHAT DO YOU THINK?

1. Thinking back on your experiences being observed, which ideas resonate with you?
2. What negatives would you add?
3. In contrast, what positives would you add?
4. What do these positives and negatives say to you as a mentor?

START-UP ISSUES: CLASSROOM MANAGEMENT FOR MENTORS

Teachers' struggles to find a path to the positives may get to the heart of most of the start-up issues you'll face when observing your mentees. No matter their intent, observers can easily come across as evaluators not mentors. When mentees feel no connection to them, view them as standing above rather than sitting beside, and see them in opposition rather than as collaborators, the affective filter goes up and any subsequent experiences are viewed through this negative lens.

Are there measures observers can take in order to come across as mentors rather than evaluators? In order to answer this question, it seems worth considering situations that face every classroom teacher and, by extension, the mentor-observer. These issues are often grouped under the broad heading of classroom management[1] or "Key teacher interventions,"[2] meaning the way the teacher organizes the students so that learning can take place. Ideas on classroom management are a good starting point for considering the role of mentors during observations. Not surprisingly, these ideas dovetail with feedback and with some of the intervention strategies discussed in Chapter 7. The observation is the time to begin managing difficult messages and facilitating reflection and mentee ownership.

Being Supportive

In his discussion on key interventions, Scrivener first notes that teachers should be supportive of class members. Similarly, a mentor should be supportive of the teacher throughout the observation whether all is going smoothly or not. To a certain extent, what supportive means is dependent on your mentees and their personal and cultural expectations. Whoever they are, however, support is more than just an inner feeling; it needs to be demonstrated in some appropriate way. This is for the sake of the teacher who is under scrutiny and also the students who may not understand properly why a stranger is present in their classroom.

Body language, especially facial expression, is one way of showing support. Having your head down constantly writing is the opposite of what your mentee may need. It may give the impression that only the occasional glance up gives the mentor a huge amount to write, and of course, the mentee could easily take this to mean that faults are being noted. Instead, looking in a friendly way around the room, at the board and the teacher could create a feeling of support.

Although praise may have different meanings to different people, part of the support your mentees are looking for is encouragement. No matter how many problems arise, the observation is also a time to note aspects of teaching that inspire admiration. Then, as you're on your way out the door—for teachers like the one in the opening illustration—or during the later debriefing, you'll have specific, planned, and genuine instances of positive feedback. Although most of the time this is quite easy, it can be challenging in a cross-cultural setting where, for example, *encouragement* may be defined as advice about how to improve. It can also be problematic in a situation that gives rise to a comment like the following: "I admired your lesson plan with its carefully thought-out stages and mixture of activities. The timing showed that you had planned this aspect well too. Let's talk about when and why you decided to abandon the plan as you went along."

In his thoughts on classroom management, Wright brings together the words "support and challenge."[3] Supporting the mentee through demeanor and praise need not preclude offering a challenge. In other words, being supportive during an observation does not mean you are required to engage exclusively in supportive interventions during feedback. Rather, it is also important to provide appropriate challenge. A balance between support and challenge will provide mentees with what they need in order to make progress through the Zone of Proximal Development (ZPD).

Being Collaborative

Wright also speaks of teachers being "responsive to learners' needs and affective states."[4] Similarly, before the observation, a mentor will have identified some of the *knowledge, skills, affect* and/or *values* needs of the teacher being observed. (See Chapter 2.) Ideally, this process occurs collaboratively when a mentee has invited a mentor into the classroom in order to give advice on a specific point. However, even when a mentor is assigned, time is limited, or a pre-observation face-to-face interaction is not possible, some collaboration, virtual or otherwise, about the teacher's needs and expectations is important. As some of our mentors working in different cross-cultural contexts have learned, this process may be begin by understanding how much individual mentees expect collaboration.

If affective needs overwhelm, collaboration may begin with a pre-observation cathartic intervention. As the opening illustration shows, mentees can have mixed emotions about being observed no matter how long they have been in the profession. For some the event is a pleasant, cooperative exercise, but for many it's disquieting. Whether in a face-to-face or virtual exchange, let the mentee put expectations and concerns into words before the lesson. You may also want to voice thoughts about what you hope to learn from the observation and your affective concerns about observing and facilitating feedback.

Collaborative observation is two-way. Like the teacher in the opening example, your mentees may appreciate the opportunity to observe you. One mentor we know rearranged her schedule so that her new teachers could observe her class during the first week of a semester. Imagine what this did for their *knowledge* and *skills* needs prior to their own first classes and their *affective* needs prior to being observed!

Being Catalytic

Another suggestion of Scrivener's is "Being catalytic."[5] He gives an example of a teacher's response when a student asks for help. The teacher guides the student to analyze the problem toward self-help. This situation is mirrored in your relationship with your mentees. A catalytic intervention starts during the observation as you note problems or details of collaboratively identified issues and consider ways to help mentees see the situation from a different perspective. Catalytic observations are especially important when your mentees, whether because of personal or cultural factors, lean toward the directive end of the feedback continuum, and careful preparation is needed before you can encourage them toward the facilitative end.

A connected idea is what Scrivener refers to as "eliciting," which he summarizes in this quote from a classroom teacher: "I think I probably tell my students lots of things that they could tell me . . . if I ever gave them the chance."[6] Mentors can fall into this trap, too, by spending the observation time writing a list of suggestions. More helpfully, they can write questions that open the door to later mentee reflection. In fact, you may want to divide your notes into two columns, one for observations about what's happening in the classroom and the other for potential questions to use during feedback. Two examples of this are included at the end of the chapter: "The Story of a Classroom" (Table 9.2) and "Teacher vs. Student Talk Time" (Table 9.3)[7] Instead of coming to conclusions, the mentor uses either form to track classroom events and prepare potential questions that will lead toward a catalytic intervention.

If you struggle to ask good questions, preparation will help. Try planning them during the observation rather than asking them unrehearsed during the debriefing (drawing on the list of question prompts you devised for Task 8.1). Then, your questions may do a better job of expressing the message you intend. They are also more likely to encourage a growth mindset and lead toward reflection and ownership. At the

Disappearing

Scrivener concludes his key interventions with a seemingly strange suggestion that the teacher should sometimes disappear from the room, although not necessarily literally. Once the students are on task, he proposes that the teacher withdraw to a corner of the classroom, for example, and let them work uninterrupted. This invisibility may be especially important for mentors who are strangers in the classroom and simply by their presence are intrusive both physically and affectively. However, you don't necessarily need to hide. In our observations in both same and cross-cultural settings, we've been asked by the teacher to pair up with a student who lacked a partner. At other times, we've quietly walked around the room and observed what students are doing during group work and have even participated in the monitoring. These experiences have been enlightening. One of our mentors took being supportive to a deeper level when she "unobtrusively" rescued a teacher from an embarrassing failure.[8] The goal of disappearing is to be inconspicuous, perhaps spending most of the class in a back corner and not interrupting normal proceedings, but it is also to be unobtrusively supportive and collaborative.

Signposting

Scrivener talks about "structuring and signposting"[9] as a way to ensure students know where learning is headed and why. Mentees, like the one in our opening example, also need to understand the purposes for observation, both the immediate outcomes and the overall direction (benchmarks you're working toward). Furthermore, they may need to be reminded that classroom observation is only one part of the mentoring process and that the wider structure includes other tasks in this section on task-based mentoring.

CHARACTERISTICS OF OBSERVATIONS

For many teachers like the ones at the start of this chapter, observations give an outside, objective view of their classrooms. As the one teacher's list of negatives suggests, however, not every approach to observation works. "In Their Own Words: Observation Approaches" reveals how two of our mentors in training attempted to figure out how to observe their mentees in appropriate ways.

IN THEIR OWN WORDS: OBSERVATION APPROACHES

As Karen and Carlos give themselves feedback, they describe their approaches to observing their mentees and explain their reasons for choosing them. It is interesting to note that they are mentoring in both same and cross-cultural settings.

Karen

Over the course of this project, you grew in the way you empathized more effectively and appropriately with a teacher you are observing. You noted that in the past you've often been very judgmental, even from the first moments of watching a teacher and making observation comments; yet by recognizing early on this tendency in yourself and using an observation tool that lent itself to more objectivity in the first observation of each teacher, you were able to consciously try to use a purer lens through which you could view these lessons . . . You have been learning how to separate your feelings from the factual things you see in the classroom and also how to look at the situation through the eyes of the mentee instead of through your own eyes . . . This is great! And I hope you will continue to grow in those skills! I can see that your tendency to focus on capturing every single detail really weighs you down when you are recording information on observation forms . . . Therefore, you need to keep the key objectives of a given observation in your mind during the whole session, to help you focus and filter out: what is worth writing down and what is excess information.

Carlos

It seems as if it is either difficult for you to give negative feedback or you just don't see some of the negative aspects of the lesson . . . Maybe as you think about future observations, think about some things that you might have seen in Teacher A's teaching that maybe she might not have realized. For example, when she is calling on students to answer questions, she usually calls on students from the front of the classroom. You could come up with an observation form that concentrates on interaction within the classroom while calling on students. Then as you present the information, it is more factual and less confrontational.

During your observation and debriefing with Teacher B, I noticed that there were other issues that entered into the formula. (Carlos explains the close relationship he has with Teacher B.) It was very clear that you felt very comfortable with her. But at the same time, during the debriefing you did not really give her much feedback. You encouraged her that she was doing a good job teaching but you really did not explain any specific points with her. Maybe the next time you observe, it would be a good idea to have something beforehand that you have talked to her about, either something that she wants you to observe about her teaching or even something that you want to observe in her teaching that you are having a problem with. [She] is a great teacher and I know you can learn a lot from her.

Karen's and Carlos's reflections on their observation practices point back to some of the start-up issues we've already discussed. Karen was particularly concerned about not being "judgmental" and instead supportive by looking through her mentees' eyes. Carlos, on the other hand, seemed to think he might need to balance support with more challenge, albeit within the context of an encouraging relationship. Carlos also wanted to collaborate with his mentees especially the second. Moreover, in their attempts to be objective, both Karen and Carlos seemed to be leaning toward catalytic observations.

Their reflections also point forward to some of the choices you have in approaching observations. The next few paragraphs look at some different characteristics of observations and distinguish them by their record, focus, timing, what is being measured, the mentor's attention, and whether they are face-to-face or virtual.

Observation Forms and Notes

Throughout the next few paragraphs, we assume that you will usually keep some sort of record of your observations. As you'll see from our examples below and samples at the end of the chapter, there are a variety of ways to do so. Another resource with a wealth of examples is Wajnryb's *Classroom Observation Tasks*.[10] In part, the format you choose is determined by your mentees, their needs, and the benchmarks you have collaboratively identified. What this means is that no single form will work perfectly with all of your mentees. In fact, all of our sample forms were designed by us or our mentors in response to the needs of our mentees. We have often tweaked each other's forms and sometimes created new. In "Now It's Your Turn," you'll have an opportunity to adapt or design your own.

Focused vs. Open-Ended

The difference between focused and open-ended observations is whether the observer is looking at a particular feature of the classroom or taking a broader view. Carlos took the first approach, wanting to create an observation form that would pinpoint details of an identified problem. In this way, he could find evidence to use in non-confrontational post-observation feedback. Although she talked about "key objectives of a given observation," Karen's reference to photography and filtering out details suggests a broader view. Rather than focusing on a particular problem, open-ended observations may reveal points that neither the mentee nor the mentor had thought about. See the two forms at the end of the chapter mentioned earlier for examples of both types of observations (focused: "Teacher vs. Student Talk Time"; open: "The Story of a Classroom").

Timing

Classroom observations can happen at any stage of the mentoring relationship, but there are different purposes at each stage.

As mentioned in Chapter 2, observations can serve as one part of a needs analysis. At times, in an early interview or informal interaction, a teacher will ask for help with a specific issue. Carlos's Teacher A might have asked for help with participation patterns, for example. At other times, the mentee might not mention any specific problems but will agree to be observed as a starting point for identifying benchmarks (an open-ended observation). That initial observation could be when Carlos first identified the need to focus on Teacher A's interaction patterns.

At the next stage, needs have already been identified. Observations will often be quite specific as you collect examples of what you and your mentee have agreed to work on. In fact, sometimes you may have to postpone further matters that could arise for discussion. Carlos and his mentee, for example, might formulate the following outcome or essential question as a means of working toward a classroom management benchmark:

1. The teacher will be able to call on a variety of students throughout a class period.
2. How can I draw all students into whole class activities?

During an observation, Carlos could then adapt one of Wajnryb's tasks to fit with Teacher A's needs and classroom context. "Managing classroom communication: interaction patterns"[11] suggests drawing a diagram of the classroom and using it to track who the teacher calls on, how often, and which students voluntarily participate.

A final observation does not always happen, but if it does, then the main purpose is to let teachers know progress that has been made and to encourage them on down the path toward mentee ownership.

Data Collection

Both Karen and Carlos wanted to be more objective and focus on facts rather than opinions. In this way, they were hoping to provide feedback that is more palatable. What they seem to be getting at is collecting data during an observation. Two general distinctions are data that is measurable numerically and what is better described in words. Measurable data could include (for items with an asterisk, you'll find observation forms at the end of the chapter):

1. The amount of talk time by the teacher (Table 9.3)★
2. Pacing or the amount of time each lesson stage took
3. How students are grouped
4. The size of groups
5. Type and/or amount of technology use
6. Wait-time between a question and answer.

In other cases, the notes will depend on more descriptive data, such as:

1. Managing errors (Table 9.4)★[12]
2. Tracking student attention (Table 9.5)★
3. Assessing learning (Table 9.6)★
4. Students' facial expressions or signs of anxiety
5. Turn-taking during group work
6. Responses to instructions.

Sometimes you may combine these two types of data collection. "Tracking Student Attention," for example, describes the level of student attention and counts the amount of time spent during each part of the lesson. Both types of data could enlighten teachers about when and why students do or do not attend.

The Mentor's Attention

Another way of approaching observations is by where the mentor's attention is focused. Wajnryb lists seven possibilities.[13] When you look through the ideas we've listed above and the sample observation forms at the end of the chapter, on which of the seven is the mentor's attention focused?

1. Learners
2. Language (of teachers and/or learners in classroom interactions)
3. Learning
4. Lesson planning and implementation
5. Teaching skills and strategies
6. Classroom management
7. Materials and resources.

Virtual Observations

As we have seen in other chapters, the mentor-mentee relationship can happen even when the two parties are in different places. Most of this chapter has been about a mentor physically visiting a classroom. However, you don't have to limit yourself to face-to-face observations. Whether or not they are possible, watching a recording of a lesson with a mentee can be an enlightening way to inspire reflection. Another option is an "unseen observation" described in some detail by Bailey.[14] Mentees come to a feedback interaction, whether face-to-face or virtual, having planned, taught, and then logged impressions or data about their teaching. Some of the observation forms at the end of the chapter can be adapted for self-observation. See, for example, "Assessing Learning: Self-Observation" (Table 9.7).

Observations can also be done using Skype or other VoIP (Voice over Internet Protocol) technology; however, the class should take precedence over the observation. When technology fails (as has happened to us), a few brief attempts to fix the problem are enough before giving up and rescheduling for another day and perhaps another mode.

OBSERVATION PLAN

Earlier in the book, you were asked to make a mentoring plan, a syllabus of sorts for your mentoring encounters. Here and in the next few chapters, you'll have an opportunity to make plans for individual encounters. Following a pattern familiar to language teachers, your observation plan has *before*, *while*, and *after* stages. In the sections below, you'll find some considerations for each stage. These are drawn from what has been talked about previously in this chapter. The "Observation Plan Template" in "Now It's Your Turn," Table 9.1 will guide you to make your own plan.

Before the Observation

Some of the anxiety the one teacher in our opening illustration experienced could have been assuaged by some pre-observation collaboration with her mentor. In either a face-to-face or virtual meeting, you and your mentees may want to negotiate some of the issues below:

1. Setting:
    - Will the observation occur physically or virtually? If virtually, what mode will be used?

- What times work for both of you?
- Which class would your mentee prefer you to observe, and why?

2. Purpose:
    - What is the purpose of the observation?
    - What do both of you hope to learn?
    - Will it be open or focused?
    - What benchmarks and specific outcomes/essential questions are being worked toward?

3. Context:
    - What is the education climate like?
    - Who are the students?
    - What are some of their obvious needs?
    - How will they react to a visitor in their class (observer effect)? What cross-cultural issues come into play?
    - What are the objectives for the observed lesson, and where does it fit into the unit/course?
    - What textbook is used?

4. Expectations:
    - What personal and cultural factors influence you and your mentee's (differing) expectations of an observation?
    - How do both of you feel about the upcoming observation? How could you help the teacher overcome any anxiety?
    - When will the teacher give you a copy of the lesson plan and any handouts?
    - Where should you sit? How should you appear to students and teacher?
    - How will you be introduced?
    - What part should you take in the lesson if any at all?
    - What will you do after class? (Is an immediate, even if brief, conversation expected?)
    - When will the debriefing take place?

5. Form/Notes
    - What will you be writing during the observation?
    - What observation form could be used, or how might one be designed?

During the Observation

What happens during the observation will largely depend on collaboration with your mentees about the questions above. By the time you are present in the classroom, you should have a plan for the following:

1. Setting: Where, when, and how (physical or virtual) will the observation take place?
2. Outcomes/Essential Questions: What one or two (probably no more) outcomes or essential questions are you and your mentee working toward, and how does this observation play a role?
3. Mentor Participation (you may have different answers to these questions for different stages of the class):
   - How will you take notes?
   - Will you use a form? If so, what form?
   - How will you otherwise participate in the class? For example, will you help to monitor group work?
4. Expectations: Although you don't necessarily need to write this down, you may also want to think through what you will do, based on pre-observation collaboration with your mentee, if something unexpected happens. How will you respond in a way that considers the needs of the learners and mentee and maintains professionalism? A list of potential unexpected moments is below.
   - A student sitting in front of you turns around mid-lesson and tries to engage you in conversation.
   - Your mentee suddenly becomes unwell.
   - Your mentee turns to you and asks, "Am I doing OK?"
   - Your mentee loses control of the class.
   - The lesson has been going well, but suddenly your mentee runs out of ideas, and the lesson comes to a halt.

After the Observation

Section III went into detail about interactive mentoring including post-observation feedback. For your observation plan, you will need to decide:

1. Setting: Where, when, and how (face-to-face or virtual) will the conversation take place? Given potential affective issues, you may want to give some thought as to what sort of ambiance would make your

mentee most comfortable while also allowing for professional (and private) discussion.
2. Main Topics/Questions: Although your observation notes/form will include this information, it may be helpful to use your plan to set up some potential structure for the interaction, including what questions you will ask in order to facilitate (rather than give) feedback.

NOW IT'S YOUR TURN

The tasks below are designed for current mentors. If you are not yet mentoring, adapt them or use them to project what you could do. For example, when completing Task 9.1, consider situations when you have observed colleagues. For Tasks 9.2 and 9.3, plan for a future mentoring encounter.

Task 9.1: Devising an Observation Approach

Some of our mentors in training have articulated personal approaches to observing mentees. Carlos, for example, might describe a Pinpointing Approach that focuses in on one aspect of a mentee's teaching. Karen's might be called a Photography Approach, as she uses a wide lens to see the class as a whole and then adjusts the aperture to focus on key aspects rather than every detail. What approach do you often take when observing mentees? What metaphor would you use to describe it? Write about your approach in your mentoring journal or share it with your mentor support group.

Task 9.2: Observation Plan

Make a plan for observing a mentee. Use the questions in "Observation Plan" above as you fill out the Observation Plan Template in Table 9.1 at the end of the chapter. Feel free to adapt the template to your mentee and her/his context.

Task 9.3: Designing an Observation Form

Design an observation form to use with your Observation Plan from Task 9.2.

1. You can use the sample forms at the end of the chapter as examples. You can also refer to Wajnryb's *Classroom Observation Tasks*.[15]

2. Collaborate with your mentee in order to adapt a form or design one of your own (in order to reach the outcomes or answer the essential questions on your Observation Plan).
3. While observing (and immediately after), decide on the best approach to using the collected data in a feedback session. Write out questions you may ask. Then, discuss the form with your mentee.
4. In your mentoring journal or with your mentor support group, assess your form and the follow-up feedback. Use the questions below as a starting point.

- How well did the form work for collecting data in the classroom?
- How well did the form work for encouraging the teacher to analyze an identified issue and make decisions about needed change?
- If you were to use this form again, how would you change it? Why?

Table 9.1 **Observation Plan Template**

BEFORE THE OBSERVATION	
Setting *(of the pre-observation meeting)*	
Location/Mode:	Time:
Questions: *What questions need to be answered before observing?*	
DURING THE OBSERVATION	
Setting *(of the observation)*	
Location/Mode:	Time:
Outcomes/Essential Questions 1. 2.	

(Continued)

Table 9.1 Continued

Mentor's participation: How will you be taking notes, what forms will be used, and/or how will you otherwise participate during each stage of the class?			
	Stages	Participation	

AFTER THE OBSERVATION			
Setting *(of the post-observation meeting)*			
Location/Mode:		Time:	
Main Topics/Questions			
	Topic	Questions	

Table 9.2 **The Story of a Classroom**

Write the *story* of what happens in the class as you observe (a summary of events, including any apt quotes from teacher or learners). In the left column, keep track of the time as events in the story unfold. In the right column, list questions you might ask in your follow-up conversation with the teacher.	
Time	Events in the story	Questions

Table 9.3 **Teacher vs. Student Talk Time**

\multicolumn{3}{l}{Keep track of the type and amount of *talk* that is taking place in the class. Note the time in the first column. In the second column, use the codes below to identify what type of *talk* is being engaged in. Write questions in the third column to ask the teacher for later analysis. Use the box at the bottom of the page to tally and to list further questions for analysis.}
TT:	Teacher Talk. The teacher is lecturing, sharing, giving instructions, etc.; the students are not speaking.	
ST:	Student Talk. Students are in pairs or groups and are interacting; the teacher is not talking.	
TST:	Teacher and Student Talk. Teacher and students are engaged in interaction, a discussion, for example.	
Q:	Quiet. Students are engaged in individual work; both the teacher and students are quiet.	
P:	Presentations. One student is giving a presentation and is the only one talking	
Duration	**Type of Talk**	**Questions**
Total	*Time*	*Percent*	*Questions*
TT:			
ST:			
TST:			
Q:			
P:			

Adapted from a form created by James A. Essert Jr.

Table 9.4 **Managing Errors**

Pay attention to how the teacher corrects learner errors and how students respond. In the last column, include questions to ask the teacher for later analysis.			
What is corrected?	*How is it corrected? (verbal/non-verbal)*	*What result? (what the learner does . . .)*	*Questions*

Adapted from a form created by Carlos.

Table 9.5 **Tracking Student Attention**

This form examines student attentiveness during different parts of a lesson and how a teacher manages problems. In the Event column, divide activities into their parts, one row per part (for example, explanation, instructions, pair practice, follow up, transition). During each part, note what students are doing that indicates attention or inattention and what the teacher does to maintain attention. Then, list questions you could later ask the teacher in order to help them analyze student attention.					
Time	*Description of Event*	*Attention Level*	*Teacher Actions*	*Questions*

Table 9.6 Assessing Learning

How is learning assessed in the classroom? In the column on the left, list objectives the teacher has identified for the lesson. While observing, keep a record of how the teacher measures whether or not objectives are being met. Describe anything the teacher does or has the students do in order to assess learning. Then list potential questions to ask the teacher for later self-analysis.		
Objectives	*Means of Assessment*	*Questions*

Table 9.7 **Assessing Learning: Self-Observation**

How do you assess learning in the classroom? In the column on the left, list your lesson objectives. After teaching, fill out the other two columns. How did you measure whether or not objectives were met? How would you analyze your assessment practices?		
Objectives	*Means of Assessment*	*Self-Analysis*

NOTES

1. Tony Wright, *Classroom Management in Language Education* (London: Palgrave Macmillan, 2005), https:/doi.org/10.1057/9780230514188.
2. Jim Scrivener, *Classroom Management Techniques* (Cambridge: Cambridge University Press, 2012), 119–178.
3. Wright, *Classroom Management in Language Education*, 173.
4. Ibid., 172.
5. Scrivener, *Classroom Management Techniques*, 154.
6. Ibid., 139.
7. This form is adapted from one created by James A. Essert Jr., a mentor we've worked with.
8. Melissa K. Smith and Marilyn Lewis, "The Language Teaching Practicum: Perspectives from Mentors," *The Teacher Trainer* 23, no. 2 (2009): 7.
9. Scrivener, *Classroom Management Techniques*, 157.
10. Ruth Wajnryb, *Classroom Observation Tasks* (Cambridge: Cambridge University Press, 1992).
11. Ibid., 106–109.
12. This form is adapted from one created by Carlos.
13. Ibid.
14. Kathleen M. Bailey, *Language Teacher Supervision* (Cambridge: Cambridge University Press, 2006), 83, https:/doi.org/10.1017/CBO9780511667329.
15. Wajnryb, *Classroom Observation Tasks*.

REFERENCES

Bailey, Kathleen M. *Language Teacher Supervision*. Cambridge: Cambridge University Press, 2006. https:/doi.org/10.1017/CBO9780511667329.

Scrivener, Jim. *Classroom Management Techniques*. Cambridge: Cambridge University Press, 2012.

Smith, Melissa K. and Marilyn Lewis. "The Language Teaching Practicum: Perspectives from Mentors." *The Teacher Trainer* 23, no. 2 (2009): 5–8.

Wajnryb, Ruth. *Classroom Observation Tasks*. Cambridge: Cambridge University Press, 1992.

Wright, Tony. *Classroom Management in Language Education*. London: Palgrave Macmillan, 2005. https:/doi.org/10.1057/9780230514188.

CHAPTER 10

Group Mentoring

WHAT DO YOU THINK?

1. Given a choice, is group or individual mentoring better?
2. What are some advantages and disadvantages to group mentoring?
3. What types of tasks especially suit group mentoring?
4. What are some considerations when planning a group mentoring task?

This book has perhaps given the impression that mentoring is a one-on-one activity. Often it is. However, at times, there is a place for group mentoring. In this chapter, you'll read about some options for tasks that can be engaged in with groups of mentees. Because group mentoring includes many potential tasks, we start with two examples to show this range. Later, we'll use the examples to illustrate two ends of a spectrum for group settings and also how to organize group tasks.

PUZZLE IT OUT: WORKSHOPS

Four mentors reflect on their experiences giving workshops. They were working with different teachers in a variety of contexts including same and cross-cultural settings and teachers of children and adults.

Cassie

I was asked to lead training sessions twice a month for all the English teachers in the department in order to improve their methodology. The main goal was to simply come alongside the teachers and generate discussions, including presentations on communicative theories and techniques, that would enable us all to learn from one another. I prepared the first session on "Teacher Motivations," using many of the questions I had previously prepared for my teacher support group last year. The outcome was very positive, as the teachers enjoyed sharing personal stories of their journey in learning English and why they became English teachers. During the term, we had good discussions on learning style differences, learning strategies, and student motivation. One experienced teacher exchanged observations with me and was very good at giving feedback and reflecting on some of her teaching practices.

Marcus

Teacher training is one of my favorite things to do as a teacher. Much of the mentoring was essentially a longer form of teacher training. One of the reasons I appreciate teacher training is that it puts theory into practice. It also allows me to fulfill my genuine desire to help people be successful at what they do, in the context in which they do it. The two experiences I had to give workshops to teachers, while only a half day in length, allowed me the opportunity to give counsel about future teaching situations. Providing resources and access to resources was the main outcome of the one training session for teachers working with primary age students, whereas discussion and direct instruction was used in the workshop I did for the other teachers. Having a half-day refresher course on topics they self-identified allowed these teachers the professional development they needed as they returned to their schools for a second year of teaching, while the email discussion that followed sporadically over the course of the semester among the workshop attendees reinforced the principles we talked about and gave the teachers a means for encouraging one another.

Karen

The local teachers with whom I had exchanged emails expressed a great interest in receiving more professional development from one or more native English speakers. Once again, I was inhibited from presenting those sessions in person, but I was able to prepare materials for another colleague to present to all the interested teachers from that school. We discussed what the teachers needed and I then wrote workshop plans with presentation materials. After I had planned materials for four complete workshops, I learned that the school administrators were not interested in having their teachers take part in those sessions and only wanted us to present a demonstration class. I then took the textbook page scans sent to me and wrote a new lesson plan with accompanying materials for my colleague to present when teaching the demonstration class to a group of seventh grade students from that local middle school. After he presented the lesson, we communicated via email about what occurred and what we could learn from that situation . . . and my colleague reported on the long list of criticisms issued by the observers, I had to tell myself not to take all of the criticisms too personally and readjust my thinking so I find some good in the situation, thereby only adding to my expertise and making me a better teacher and mentor.

Rachel

The assessment workshop was for all teachers teaching in my city. I felt a little inadequate when I presented this session. Assessment is not always my strongest area as a teacher, so I made the session less lecture style and decided to offer some basic principles for on-going assessment and then have the teachers discuss what they have done, what they would be willing to try from a list I offered, and challenged them to try one new method and reflect. I wished there could have been a follow up, but time and availability are limited. There was one teacher who came to me later asking for advice and help in creating and using portfolios. That was rewarding, and I felt like my efforts had been useful for at least one teacher. I was also able to see how impractical some of my advice had been in the session. If I were to do this session again, I would have done it differently and included more samples rather than theoretical ideas.

HERE'S WHAT HAPPENED: A TEACHER SUPPORT GROUP

In Chapters 4 and 5, you read about a support group with Chinese English teachers. Here, one of us (Melissa) describes how the group began as a conversation practice for colleagues and then inadvertently developed into a teacher support group. Her reflections below include quotes from participants in the group.

Inspired by a friend's enthusiasm for learning English and teaching, I decided to start a Teachers English Corner for colleagues at my university in China. It would include English conversation practice with a double purpose of developing our passion for English and teaching. We started informally, meeting over lunch or in my home. The semi-structured discussions often focused on teaching but sometimes on the culture of English-speaking countries (We voted in a US presidential election and celebrated American Thanksgiving, for example.), or life (how to communicate better with family members).

As I drew on my colleagues' input and refined Teachers English Corner, it gradually developed into a teacher support group in two different ways. First, *the relationships between members grew in such a way that support became a defining characteristic of the group. The original members formed their own in-group, and then new members were welcomed and made to feel like insiders. Participants described the group as "friendly," "inviting," "warm," and "relaxing." They seemed to see it as a safe place to try out new language and solve (classroom) problems.*

Secondly, the group became a place of collaborative professional development. The teachers saw it as a space for "learning from each other" and of the "exchange" of "perspectives," "experiences," and "ideas." They found this sharing helpful, and even when describing the atmosphere of English Corner used words/phrases like "professional," "enlightening," and "keeping up with the pace of education changes."

Teachers English Corner continues to be refined. Most recently, trying to keep up with the pace of change, we focused on six trends in education. Each week ten Chinese and American teachers from five different schools met in order to discover a trend together. Each face-to-face discussion was followed up by a blog post which included online resources and an individual task to try something new and report back to our closed group on social media. Face-to-face and virtual interactions were used to encourage each other (in teaching and sometimes also life) to try new techniques for the sake of our students, but also as a way to breathe fresh air into our profession.

WHAT DO YOU THINK?

If you want to enter into the spirit of this section, discuss your answers to the questions below with your mentor support group.

1. As you read through "Puzzle It Out: Workshops" and "Here's What Happened: A Teacher Support Group," what advantages and disadvantages to group mentoring stood out?
2. What steps did these mentors take to face some of the challenges? What else could they have done?
3. What steps did they take to remedy some of the weaknesses? What else could they have done?
4. Which of these two group frameworks could you use with teachers you mentor? How might you need to adapt it?
5. If you were giving advice to mentors or mentees about using group tasks as part of the mentoring relationship, what would you include?

ADVANTAGES AND DISADVANTAGES OF GROUP MENTORING

One of the greatest advantages of group mentoring may be efficiency. When two mentees, for example, were teaching the same material and type of students and struggling with similar issues, meeting together with them for feedback sessions saved time. When a group of mentees were all teaching in a similar setting unfamiliar to their mentor, she set up a panel discussion featuring teachers from a variety of similar situations. Many of the mentees' questions were answered during the ninety-minute block, and then afterward they approached different teachers on the panel for one-on-one interaction. Some of our mentors have also co-led workshops and support groups, doubling efficiency when the responsibility for mentoring the group was shared.

Although an efficient way to interact and help mentees answer questions, there are other considerations before deciding on a group rather than an individual task. Many of the advantages and disadvantages described below expand on points raised in other places in this book.

Mentoring Relationship

At the beginning of this book, we emphasized the importance of relationship to the mentoring process and throughout the book have assumed that mentoring is occurring within the context of genuine and collaborative relationships. In group settings, investing in relationships with individual mentees may be challenging. In fact, the impersonal nature of group frameworks seemed to bother some of the mentors in "Puzzle It Out: Workshops." At least it is interesting to note that two of the four specifically mentioned individual teachers who sought them out later for one-on-one interactions that lead to some form of deeper relationship, and a third commented on how the group continued to interact virtually in a way that was mutually encouraging.

In some situations, however, a group relationship may work just as well or better than one-on-one. When teachers are not naturally introspective, a group setting can inspire them toward reflection as they see it done by others. Furthermore, in a framework like the one described in "Here's What Happened: A Teacher Support Group," mentees might be more comfortable and less inhibited when they can learn teaching with the support of an in-group.

Group mentoring may also have a positive effect on relationships within an entire program. Katie, a teacher in an English language program for refugees in the United States, spoke gratefully of the weekly teacher meetings their supervisor facilitates in order to generate ideas and develop curriculum. In a professional environment that values mutual respect and encouragement, these weekly collaborations seem to be a natural extension of their harmonious relationships that also encompass interactions with students in and outside the classroom. The students seem inspired by this model. Katie described the pleasure of watching a student from one part of the world teach (and encourage) a student from a completely different background. The teachers' relationships have inspired the students, or perhaps it's vice versa.

Affective Filter

While none of the mentors we know would purposefully shame their mentees, there is potential for unintended embarrassment in group settings. Even when an issue belongs to the group, mentees may feel singled out if they assume the problem is theirs alone. However, what is more likely is that the group will provide a safe venue for needed interactions with a teacher. Through a group task, you may be able to broach a sensitive issue in a non-threatening way. It can be addressed as an issue many in the group are struggling with or as part of a larger category of challenges others are facing. Mentees may be more open to reflection and ownership when they see that they are not alone in their struggle and as they collaborate with peers.

The director of an intensive English program at a university in the United States explained how the newest and least experienced members of their staff (though trained mentors) had been invited to lead a teacher support group. While attending a presentation one of them gave, she'd realized that mentoring is non-threatening. Specifically, she saw that observations can be for developmental rather than evaluative purposes, issues can be self-identified, and growth self-monitored. Now, monthly teacher meetings in their program also include an innovative professional development component facilitated by the two mentors (with less than ten years of experience each), and their colleagues with ten, twenty, and thirty years of experience are engaging together, without fear, in peer observation, reflection on teaching practices, discussions about articles and second language learning theories, and analysis of case studies.

One-Way Transmission vs. Collaborative Dialog

At the beginning of Chapter 8, we highlighted a note from Malderez[1] in which she observed problems with the term *giving feedback* because it suggests one-way transmission rather than collaborative dialog. Some of the same issues come into play with group mentoring. We talk about *giving* workshops or trainings. Even when leading a discussion group, the temptation to transmit may interfere with collaboration. You see this dilemma in "Puzzle It Out: Workshops" where the mentors use words and phrases like *present, direct instruction, offer,* and *provide,* and at the same time talk about *discussion, practice, try,* and *reflect.*

On the other hand, collaboration may be richer in a group setting. Teachers in Cassie's workshops were able to "learn from one another." The virtual interactions that followed Marcus's training gave his teachers "a means for encouraging one another." Moreover, the "learning from each other" and exchange of ideas in Teachers English Corner was between all members of the group. In Katie's setting, collaboration seems to characterize work, professional development, and even life.

One of our mentors purposely used a group setting in order to encourage greater collaboration between teachers at her university in China. Modeling what she was hoping for, she and a Chinese colleague cooperated in order to set up a series of peer observations in which each expatriate teacher observed a local teacher and vice versa. "The outcome was increased collaboration between the two groups and a step towards self-directed professional development."[2]

GROUP SETTINGS

Richards and Farrell[3] list a number of group settings through which professional development can occur, including workshops and teacher support groups as well as peer observation, peer coaching, and team teaching. Although many of these group activities can be engaged in by teachers, in this chapter the focus is on mentor-facilitated group tasks. These tasks can be accomplished in a range of settings. We look at these settings by grouping them into two broad categories with the understanding that there can be overlap between the two (see Figure 10.1). On one end would be something like a workshop or training session, and on the other, a group discussion, perhaps a teacher support group or a collaborative group like Katie's.

Group settings can range from formal, in a classroom-type venue, to an informal get-together in an office, over lunch, or possibly in someone's home. They may reach a large group of mentees, even as many as fifty to one hundred teachers in a workshop, for example. Teacher support or collaborative groups, on the other hand, may consist of ten or fewer mentees. Because of the larger group and the formal framework, workshops are often more structured than discussion groups. This is not to say that mentors are less prepared for discussion groups. Rather questions or tasks are carefully planned out; however, there is more flexibility to adapt based on how the conversation flows. In formal situations, mentors may be literally *on stage*. This does not mean, however, that they are *on*

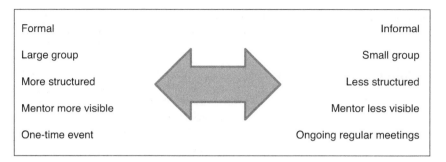

Figure 10.1 Group Settings for Task-Based Mentoring

stage figuratively. Rather than transmitting information to their audience, they are more visible as they manage activities in large group settings. In discussion groups, mentors are less visible, possibly asking a question and then letting the group take over. Although they may participate in the answer, they do so not as an expert but as a peer. Finally, workshops are often one-time events or possibly a series of two or three. Discussion groups are usually held regularly over a period of time.

VIRTUAL GROUP SETTINGS

Group mentoring can also be facilitated in virtual settings. When choosing modes of communication from all the options available, the considerations mentioned in Chapter 7 come into play in a special way. Convenience becomes more complicated when you have to fit the lifestyle of a group of mentees. An asynchronous task, for example, would work better than synchronous with a number of teachers spread across several time zones with varying qualities of internet connection. When considering convenience and also how to establish and maintain relationship, you may find that a combination of face-to-face and virtual works well.

Rather than listing possible modes of virtual communication for group tasks, the paragraphs below contain examples of settings that are either virtual or include online tools. In some cases, they elaborate on situations you read about above or in other places in this book.

Workshops

One of Marcus's workshops in "Puzzle It Out: Workshops" was followed up by an email discussion. Another mentor has held live workshops that are then summarized and posted, with pictures and video clips, to a closed group on social media. A third mentor has used video clips and animated multimedia presentations combined with tasks and follow-up discussion forums to facilitate asynchronous virtual workshops.

Teacher Support Groups

Although the group described in "Here's What Happened: Teacher Support Groups" primarily met face-to-face, it was supplemented in virtual ways. One week, for example, participants met to discover *grit*[4] by completing a "grit scale,"[5] deciding on what the concept entails, and figuring out how it might apply in their classrooms. These face-to-face discussions were followed up by a blog post with linked resources like Duckworth's TED Talk on grit,[6] and an individual task to help their students develop grit. (Some participants reported back to our closed social media group on a listening lesson they designed for students using Duckworth's TED Talk.)

Collaborative Groups

As part of her ongoing mentoring, Sarah led a project with a group of her mentees in which they performed a needs analysis of their students—refugees in the Middle East who were awaiting placement in other countries. With Sarah in one country and her mentees in another, they designed surveys, interviewed students and teachers (from current and future settings), devised learner profiles, and analyzed data. They held meetings using Skype or engaged in group email discussions. They used file sharing for instrument design and data analysis. The structure Sarah designed into the needs analysis project balanced out some of the challenges she'd faced in previous virtual settings with these mentees. The completion of the project depended on each teacher's participation. This added a level of accountability to the relationship. As the project progressed and mentees saw how it could better their teaching, their motivation increased as did their positive attitudes toward professional development as a whole.

GROUP TASK PLAN

In the last chapter, you made an observation plan. In this chapter, you have an opportunity to make a group task plan. (See Task 10.3 in "Now It's Your Turn" and the template in Table 10.2.) Group mentoring tasks often occur within a larger framework like the settings, whether face-to-face or virtual, discussed above. The paragraphs below and the template will first help you to situate group mentoring inside a broader framework. Then, you will plan for a specific task within that setting.

Framework

You've been given a variety of options for group settings, both face-to-face and virtual. The questions below will help you to collaborate with your group and determine which framework is most appropriate.

1. Setting:
    - What setup works best for the group (formal or informal, more or less structured, one-time or regular meetings)?
    - How will the group meet (face-to-face and/or virtual)?
    - If face-to-face, where will the group meet?
    - If virtual, what mode(s) of communication will be used?
    - When and how often will the group meet?
2. Expectations/Goals:
    - What is the purpose of the group?
    - What do mentees expect to give to and gain from the group?
    - What are their expectations of you and your participation?
    - What are their needs?
    - What are the overall goals, or what benchmarks are you working toward?

Task

Within the group framework, you also have options for how you will facilitate tasks. The questions below will guide your planning for one task.

1. Setting: Where, when, and how will this particular task take place?
2. Outcomes/Essential Questions: In order to reach the benchmarks identified above, what smaller steps (outcomes or essential questions) does your group need to work toward?
    - Which of those are they ready to focus on?
    - What task might help them reach some of the outcomes or answer essential questions?
3. Procedures:
    - As you consider how to reach outcomes or answer essential questions, what procedure(s) will you follow during the group task? Some possibilities are compiled below from the examples above and other situations. Note that although some of these are either face-to-face or virtual, many of them can be both.

- Discussion or online forum
- Panel discussion
- Reflection
- Analysis or evaluation
- Demonstration
- Role play or simulation
- Discovery learning
- Blog
- Collaborative needs analysis, lesson planning, or curriculum development
- Practice
- Team teaching
- Peer observation
- Peer coaching or peer mentoring[7]
- Action research (we'll talk about this more in the next chapter).
  - What steps will you follow in order to facilitate the chosen procedure(s)?
4. Materials:
   - What materials best support the steps for the procedure(s)? Some possibilities are compiled below.
     - Samples (of lesson plans, textbooks, resources, etc.)
     - Case studies
     - Articles, blog posts, or books
     - Surveys, questionnaires, or online polls[8]
     - Websites
     - Video clips (of brief talks or classroom teaching)
     - Multimedia presentations
     - Observation forms. (See the example of a peer observation form in Table 10.3 at the end of the chapter. The forms discussed in the last chapter could also be adapted.)

Follow Up

Once a particular task is completed, your group will likely need to get together, face-to-face or virtually, in order to reflect or report on what they have learned.

1. Setting: Where, when, and how will the follow up take place?
2. Procedures/Materials: What procedures and materials (possibly from the lists above) will be used during the follow up?

NOW IT'S YOUR TURN

The tasks below are designed for current mentors. If you are not yet mentoring, use them to project what you might do. For example, Task 10.1, steps 1 and 2 could be completed with potential mentees in mind and then used as a topic for your mentoring journal. Task 10.3 could be a plan for a future mentoring encounter that you share with your mentor support group.

Task 10.1: Choosing a Group Setting

Consider how well task-based mentoring in a group setting would work for your current or future mentees and then decide which setting would work best for them.

1. Based on your mentees and their needs and your mentoring context, consider the advantages and disadvantages of different group settings. Table 10.1 lists three of the possibilities introduced in this chapter. Feel free to make them more specific. For example, you could list three types of collaborative groups (for peer observation, curriculum development, or needs analysis). You can also add other group settings in the empty rows. Then, brainstorm for the pros and cons of using each setting with your mentees.
2. Based on your brainstorming, narrow down your choices. Select two to three that would work well with a group of your mentees.
3. Choose three to five mentees in your potential group, share your ideas with them, and ask which setting they would most likely participate in.

Table 10.1 **Advantages and Disadvantages of Group Settings**

	Advantages	Disadvantages
Workshop		
Teacher support group		
Collaborative group		

Task 10.2: Group Mentoring Proposal

Based on what you learn from Task 10.1, choose one group setting. Write a brief proposal or advertisement about the group to send to potential participants. (Note that a prerequisite to this task may be sending a proposal to your mentees' institution(s) and asking for permission to facilitate such a group.) Include the following in your proposal/advertisement:

1. A brief description of the group, including its purpose and what will take place
2. Meeting times and location or mode
3. A specific date by which they should respond and commit to participating
4. At this point, you could also ask mentees for input about potential tasks to complete in your group.

Task 10.3: Group Task Plan

Use the template below and the questions and guidelines in this chapter (specifically in the "Group Task Plan" section) in order to plan a task to complete with your mentoring group. Feel free to adapt the template to suit your mentees and setting.

Table 10.2 Group Task Plan Template

FRAMEWORK	
Setting	
Group Setup:	
Locations/Modes:	Dates/Time
Goals/Benchmarks: *What overall goals is the group working toward, or which benchmarks?*	
TASK	
Setting	
Location/Mode:	Time:
Outcomes/Essential Questions 1. 2. 3.	

Procedures and Materials			
	Procedures	Materials	

FOLLOW UP			
Setting			
Location/Mode:		Time:	
Procedures and Materials			
	Procedures	Materials	

Table 10.3 **Peer Observation Form**

Observe another teacher in our group. As you observe, answer the questions below. Keep in mind that the purpose of these questions is to help you develop as a teacher and not to evaluate the teacher you're observing.

1. What's one aspect of teaching we've discussed in our group that you see at work in this classroom? Describe what you see and how it relates to our discussions.

2. List and describe one or two behaviors or techniques engaged in by the teacher that you would like to try in your own teaching and explain why.

3. Take a few minutes (twenty or more) and observe the students' facial expressions, actions, and responses to directions, explanations, and pair/group work. What do you notice about their comprehension and engagement? What else do you notice about these learners?

4. Suppose that you will be teaching these students next week. Based on what you learned from observing them, how would you go about designing a lesson for them?

NOTES

1. Angi Malderez, "Mentoring," in *The Cambridge Guide to Second Language Teacher Education*, ed. Anne Burns and Jack C. Richards (Cambridge: Cambridge University Press, 2009), Kindle edition.
2. Robin Schmidt and Xianwen Song, "One Degree of Change: Exploring Attitudes about Observation and Collaboration," *TESOL Theory and Praxis* 2, no. 1 (2017): 1.
3. Jack C. Richards and Thomas S. C. Farrell, *Professional Development for Language Teachers* (Cambridge: Cambridge University Press, 2005).
4. Angela Lee Duckworth, *Grit: The Power of Passion and Perseverance* (New York: Scribner, 2016).
5. Angela Lee Duckworth, "Grit Scale," *Angela Duckworth*, 2017, http://angeladuckworth.com/grit-scale/.
6. Angela Lee Duckworth, "Grit: The Power of Passion and Perseverance," Filmed April 2013, TED video, 6:12, www.ted.com/talks/angela_lee_duckworth_grit_the_power_of_passion_and_perseverance?language=en.
7. Christopher Stillwell, "The Collaborative Development of Teacher Training Skills," *ELT Journal* 63, no. 4 (2009), 353–362, https:/doi.org/10.1093/elt/ccn068.
8. See, for example, www.polleverywhere.com/.

REFERENCES

Duckworth, Angela Lee. "Grit: The Power of Passion and Perseverance." Filmed April 2013. TED video, 6:12. www.ted.com/talks/angela_lee_duckworth_grit_the_power_of_passion_and_perseverance?language=en.

Duckworth, Angela Lee. *Grit: The Power of Passion and Perseverance.* New York: Scribner, 2016.

Duckworth, Angela Lee. "Grit Scale." *Angela Duckworth.* 2017. http://angeladuckworth.com/grit-scale/.

Malderez, Angi. "Mentoring." In *Cambridge Guide to Second Language Teacher Education*, edited by Anne Burns and Jack C. Richards, Chapter 26. Cambridge: Cambridge University Press, 2009. Kindle edition.

Richards, Jack C. and Thomas S. C. Farrell. *Professional Development for Language Teachers.* Cambridge: Cambridge University Press, 2005.

Schmidt, Robin and Xianwen Song. "One Degree of Change: Exploring Attitudes about Observation and Collaboration." *TESOL Theory and Praxis* 2, no. 1 (2017): 1–11.

Stillwell, Christopher. "The Collaborative Development of Teacher Training Skills." *ELT Journal* 63, no. 4 (2009): 353–362. https:/doi.org/10.1093/elt/ccn068.

CHAPTER 11

Action Research Projects

WHAT DO YOU THINK?

1. When you hear the phrase *action research*, what ideas come to mind? What feelings does it evoke?
2. What are some potential benefits to using action research as a mentoring task?
3. How many options are there for planning action research?
4. What do you need to learn or do in order to facilitate an action research project with a mentee?

After facilitating an action research project with a group of mentees, Rachel had this to say: "I loved doing that project. It has been a pivotal part of my experience in fact. I am so thankful that those teachers were willing to participate so wholeheartedly for me—and for them."

In this section on task-based mentoring, Chapter 9 talked about observation, which is often seen as the primary task mentors engage in with their mentees. Then, Chapter 10 gave you an opportunity to prepare for group mentoring tasks. This chapter's focus—action research projects—may not initially be viewed, by you or your mentees, in the positive way in which Rachel saw her project. Action research may be the least common approach to professional development or perhaps the one considered most difficult. Moreover, it's not necessarily seen as a mentor-facilitated task, and when it is, mentors may be less confident than they are engaging in other tasks. As you read "Here's what happened: Facilitating Action Research Projects," consider how you might respond in a similar situation.

HERE'S WHAT HAPPENED: FACILITATING ACTION RESEARCH PROJECTS

Participants in a mentor training program were asked to look at the following course outcomes and decide which seemed most interesting and which most challenging. Although participants chose a variety of outcomes that sounded interesting, most of them included challenges from the affect category.

Table 11.1 Outcomes for a Mentoring Course

1. Knowledge:
   - Describe aspects of the classroom that pose challenges for inexperienced teachers.
   - Explain methods for researching the classroom.
   - State reasons why classroom research is helpful for in-service teachers.
2. Skills:
   - Help in-service teachers develop, implement, and understand action research projects.
   - Lead in-service teachers to make changes to their teaching based on what you learn from classroom research.
   - Implement classroom research projects with local teachers in a way that is culturally appropriate.
3. Affect:
   - Feel enthusiastic about planning and implementing classroom research.
   - Realize that classroom research is manageable for mentors and mentees.

WHAT DO YOU THINK?

1. Which outcomes sound most interesting to you? Why?
2. Which sound most worthwhile?
3. Which outcomes sound most challenging to you? Why?
4. Does facilitating an action research project seem more challenging to you than other mentoring tasks? Why? What would make it seem more manageable?

ACTION RESEARCH PROJECTS   167

One reason why facilitating an action research project may seem more challenging than other mentoring tasks is that you aren't sure how to do one yourself, let alone lead a mentee through it. The purpose of this chapter is to help you facilitate action research in part by making it seem feasible (and feel doable) to you.

Let's start with a definition that makes research sound manageable: "Research is merely systematic inquiry that is undertaken when a person runs into a difficulty or simply becomes curious and seeks to learn more about an object, situation, or phenomenon."[1] Some of the features included in TESOL (Teaching English to Speakers of Other Languages) inquiry are listed below.[2]

1. Classroom-based or classroom-oriented
2. Done by or with classroom teachers
3. Outcome-based
4. Flexible in design
5. Context-driven and case-based
6. Self-empowered.

For the purpose of this chapter, we would add that action research can be a mentor-facilitated task for learning teaching whereby a mentor and mentee(s) collaboratively identify and solve problems through classroom-based inquiry.

WHY ACTION RESEARCH

Before digging into the details, consider why you and your mentee may want or need to engage in an action research project. Back in Chapter 9, we talked about how mentees and mentors may first need to clear out negative feelings about observations before engaging in them as a mentoring task. Participating in action research may also be a process that begins by clearing out the negatives so that you can see the purpose. The questions in "What Do You Think?" below will take you (and your mentee) through the initial steps toward identifying a purpose for action research.

WHAT DO YOU THINK?

1. Affective Issues: How do you and your mentee feel about engaging in action research? Which of the words below describe your feelings? Which might describe the feelings of your mentee? What other words would you use?

- Nervous
- Uninterested
- Willing
- Needing some ideas
- Confident
- Excited.

2. Benefits: If either of you is struggling with affective issues related to research, you could identify some of the benefits you both may gain. A few possibilities are below. Which would you choose for yourself? Which would your mentee choose? What would either of you add?
   - A problem is put into words as one step in solving it.
   - You've been informally researching something in the classroom and would like to consider it more thoroughly and formally.
   - You already have classroom data from another mentoring task and would like to understand better what it means.
   - A success seems worth celebrating by studying how it came about.
   - You think others might be able to learn from what you have gained from another mentoring task.
   - You develop professionally.
   - Presenting at a conference or publishing a paper is a requirement for your job or something you would like to try (again).

3. Potential directions: One way to become more excited about action research is to consider possible directions you and your mentee could go. In other words, what are some of the problems you have collaboratively identified that could be solved through classroom-based inquiry (or by looking at observation or other data you've collected as part of your mentoring interactions)?

TYPES OF RESEARCH

Another way to cultivate a positive view of action research is to consider manageable ways of approaching it. Action research is done for the purpose of experimenting with steps, during the process, to solve problems and make learning better for students. In mentor-facilitated action research, the burden of experimentation and problem-solving is shared because the project is done collaboratively rather than individually. In fact, it could be done as a group mentoring task although a smaller group might work better. (If it is published, for example, more than four names under one article would be rare.)

Table 11.2 **Qualitative and Quantitative Research**

	Qualitative	Quantitative
Data	Non-numerical, descriptive	Uses numbers and statistics
Questions Answered	What kind of . . .?	How much . . .?
	In what way . . .?	How many . . .?
Example	Case studies	Surveys

Action research can be conducted in a number of different ways. Types are often stated as opposites, and many overlap. One of the most common distinctions, for example, is between qualitative and quantitative research. Table 11.2 illustrates the differences between the two. Case studies are usually qualitative and surveys quantitative. Program evaluation may include elements of both.

Types of research can also be categorized as general or specific, learner- or teacher-focused, replicated or original, and short- or long-term. An action research project will often combine features from several of these different types. Four resources are listed below where you can find more information about types of research and some of the challenges you may face in conducting a research project.

1. *Doing Second Language Research*[3]
2. *Research Methods in Applied Linguistics*[4]
3. *Continuum Companion to Research Methods in Applied Linguistics*[5]
4. *Doing Research in Applied Linguistics: Realities, Dilemmas and Solutions.*[6]

Some different types of research are described in more detail below. The list is not exhaustive because our primary purpose here is not to introduce action research but to expose you to it as a means of task-based mentoring and supporting teachers' professional development. Accordingly, we've focused on types that our mentors in training have chosen to engage in because they were a feasible way for their mentees to learn teaching. You also may find them doable for you and your mentees. In order to show how they might work as a mentoring task, we've included examples of projects our mentors have facilitated with their mentees. Notice how some of them incorporated more than one type into their projects.

CASE STUDIES

In a case study, the researcher observes the characteristics of a person, a group of students, a class etc., using descriptive data from more than one source (for example, teacher reflections, lesson plans, students' work, observation notes, and/or interviews). In a mentor-facilitated action research project, case studies are easily managed because they use data that already exists (from previous mentoring encounters) or is easily obtained because the people being studied are your mentee and her/his students (and sometimes also you, the mentor). In this way, case studies also fulfill the purpose of collaboratively identifying and solving problems.

> **Cassie's Project**: *The purpose of this study was to explore the differences and outcomes between Chinese and foreign teachers' approaches to implementing communicative tasks in an EFL context in China. Reciprocal observations were done between one American mentor and each of three Chinese teachers, and an observation form designed for the purpose of the study was used. After individual post-observation meetings, each teacher also filled out a follow-up reflection form. Teachers were encouraged to use what they observed and learned in order to make their classes more interactive (specifically by asking questions from the deeper levels of Bloom's Taxonomy). Results were shared in meetings with a larger group of mentees.*

SURVEY RESEARCH

Surveys aim to find out answers without the researcher having to travel to different places and by hearing from a larger group of responders than is possible with other methods. Data is collected through written questionnaires and/or by interviews. Because interviews can be conducted by email or Skype and surveys set up online (using a Google Form, for example), they may be an easy means of facilitating an action research project if you and your mentees are at a distance.

> **Sandra and Carlos's Project**: *This study set out to answer two questions: (1) Do EFL students in a private language school in Central Asia have a positive or negative attitude toward native language usage in their classroom? (2) Do students of different proficiency and age have different views about the importance of the native language? Two North American mentors worked with one local teacher in order to design, translate, and administer a survey to students. Then, the three observed each other's use of the students' native language in the classroom and came up with a plan of action for when and how to do so appropriately. Findings were shared at a workshop for local teachers on the topic: "Use of L1 in L2 Classroom as Lubricant to Keep the Wheels Running Smoothly."*

NARRATIVE RESEARCH

Because defining narrative research is somewhat complex, it may be easiest to describe it by what it does. It combines storytelling and research; stories become data or are used to analyze and report data.[7] This type of research might work well when you're mentoring a teacher who is naturally reflective. The process of articulating a story (your mentee's or her/his students') or using storytelling to examine data could also be a means of developing mentees' reflective abilities. Barkhuizen's edited collection of narrative research[8] would make an interesting starting point if you are interested in investigating language learning and teaching with your mentees through this method.

> **Melody's Project**: *The study was part of a larger project exploring how the experiences of language teachers shaped the development of their convictions and attitudes toward teaching and learning. A series of interviews and classroom observations were completed with each teacher, and then their stories were written. For one of the teachers in particular, the process of being observed, interviewed, and narrated cycled back around to her classroom practices as she reflected and articulated her story. She viewed our interviews as an opportunity for professional development and spoke gratefully of how she had benefited through the process.*

PROGRAM EVALUATION

After a program has been held or sometimes during, people want to know how effective it is, including the financial sponsors, the institution where it is held, and the teachers themselves. To find answers, the researchers systematically collect and analyze information so as to judge the effectiveness of the program and suggest improvements. Because your mentees are primary stakeholders where they teach, program evaluation may provide a meaningful approach to your action research with them. The data you collect may come from interviewing administrators or other teachers, asking questions of learners, looking at examination results or other student work, and/or doing classroom observations.

> **Sarah's Project**: *Although set up as a needs analysis project, the study included elements of program evaluation. In order to determine the needs of their students—refugees awaiting placement in other countries, the mentees attempted to understand the existing program. With help from their mentor, they observed classes, interviewed and surveyed students and teachers, and*

then compared what they learned with online interview data from teachers and administrators from refugee programs in potential placement countries. At the end of the study, the mentees designed a scope and sequence to guide their attempts to prepare learners for future placement.

RESEARCH SYNTHESIS

This type is sometimes called library research in contrast to primary research (involving collecting original data). In this case, the investigator brings together research from a number of sources through a summary, which is sometimes called a state-of-the-art review. Such reviews are helpful in letting future researchers know what has already been found out and what questions are waiting to be answered. In an action research project, a research synthesis provides you and your mentee with potential solutions to the problem you've identified by looking at how others have solved it.

> **Bertie's Project**: *The purpose of this project was to explore problems with classroom management. The mentee first identified and analyzed specific problems and potential causes. The mentor, then, using a form designed in collaboration with the mentee, observed the problem class in order to see what was really happening and if there was a pattern to particular problems. (For example, were they occurring when the teacher was presenting information or during practice?) Journal articles were consulted in order to identify possible solutions. Steps—new lesson planning decisions and changes in teaching behaviors—were implemented by the teacher until she felt more confident managing her classroom.*

COMPLETING PROJECTS AT A DISTANCE

Before getting into the specifics of your action research project, let's open the door one more time to virtual mentoring. As with every other task we've discussed in these last three chapters, action research projects can be completed face-to-face or at a distance. In fact, action research projects may be more easily accomplished virtually than many other tasks. We know this in part because almost all of our research and writing has been completed while one of us was in New Zealand and the other in China (and sometimes the United States) with the occasional meeting in a fourth country. In different ways, we have taken turns mentoring each other through parts of the process. We also know this because some of the examples we included above were facilitated by mentors in one place while their mentees were in another. As you read the paragraphs below and begin to make your action research plan, keep the door open to virtually mentoring your teacher(s) through part or all of your project. Given location, time, and personal preferences, what modes of communication will work best for facilitating an action research project with your mentee(s)?

ACTION RESEARCH PLAN

The following paragraphs will take you through the steps of facilitating an action research project and guide you in making an action research plan. While you read (and begin to plan), you can refer to the Action Research Plan Template in Table 11.4 at the end of the chapter.

What is not included on the template is a place for resources. They may be better kept in a shared document or folder that both you and your mentee contribute to (perhaps an expansion of the resource folder you started in Task 4.4). Then, at various phases throughout the project, research that has already been done (and published) will provide needed background information or direction. Before beginning actual research, these studies can guide you and your mentee as you choose from potential topics, formulate research questions, and select methods. If you decide to present or publish your project, the articles may become part of your literature review. See Task 11.1 for more information.

Framework

Before beginning your action research project, you have some decisions to make in collaboration with your mentee(s). The following considerations and questions will guide you as you set up your project.

1. Setting:
    - Which of your mentees will you be collaborating with for this project? (Consider who is ready for or may benefit most from action research.)
    - How will the collaboration occur? For example, will you meet regularly? How often, and when? Will the meetings be face-to-face or virtual?
2. Outcomes/Essential Questions:
    - Which benchmarks for teachers will you aim toward through an action research project?

- In order to reach benchmarks, what outcomes are you planning to work toward, or what essential questions will the project answer? (This is where you and your mentee collaboratively identify the problem to be studied—and then solved—through classroom-based inquiry.)

3. Topic: The topic you choose will be drawn from the outcomes or essential questions you're working toward. Some other considerations are included below. (Referring to your resource folder may help to answer some of these questions.)

    - What topic are you and your mentee personally interested in?
    - What topic is realistic given your time frame and situation?
    - In the setting (and society) you're working in, what is appropriate? What is ethical? If you need permission for research, what topic is likely to work?
    - What topic fits with current trends in TESOL?
    - Which one is likely to be published or accepted for presentation at a conference?
    - Which will help your mentee reach professional development requirements set by her/his institution (possibly for promotion)?

4. Research Question or Hypothesis: Once you've decided on an area of interest, the next step is for you and your mentee to word your research question or hypothesis (assuming you have an idea about a possible result). One place to begin is your outcomes/essential questions where you have already identified the problem you want to study. Another way to think about the wording of your question/hypothesis is to analyze the way the studies in your shared resource folder introduce their research. Task 11.2 in "Now It's Your Turn" will take you and your mentee through this analysis.

5. Method: Choosing a topic and the best way of exploring it are closely linked. The next section goes into more detail about how you and your mentee will collect and analyze data. At this point, consider:

    - What overall method fits best with your topic? (Refer to "Types of Research" above or to studies in your resource folder.)
    - What data will you need to collect, and how could you collect it?

Researching

1. Data Collection: Your study may draw on data that already exists (from previous mentoring interactions), or you and your mentee may need to collect data.

- What sources of data will you draw from, or what investigation procedures will you follow? Some possible data sources/investigation procedures are listed below. In addition, the articles in your resource folder will give you and your mentee other ideas.
    - Observations: You and your mentee could adapt or design an observation form, possibly one from Chapter 9, that collects data to answer your research question. Then, you observe her/him (and s/he may observe you).
    - Recordings (either audio or video of a class or part of a class taught by your mentee)
    - Journals (kept by your mentee reflecting on certain aspects of teaching)
    - Samples (of lessons plans, students' work, etc.)
    - Interviews (of students or other teachers)
    - Questionnaires (administered to students, other teachers, stakeholders in a program, etc.).
- Where and when will data be collected?

2. Analysis: Because there are many different ways to analyze data (depending on the type), one of the best ways to decide what to do with your data is for you and your mentee to examine how it was analyzed in the studies in your resource folder. Some questions that might also help are listed below.
    - What trends do you see in the data?
    - Are there any sudden breaks with patterns? What do the breaks mean?
    - What are some different ways or possible measures you could use to explain what you see in the data?

Using Results

The purpose of action research is to identify and solve problems. Thus, the primary way your mentee will use the results is to take action on what you learned through your study. As Farrell expresses it, "The final steps in the cycle of action research [are] . . . deciding on some type of action, monitoring the effects of that action and, if necessary, problem redefinition."[9] However, there is no need to stop there. The questions below give ideas about how you and your mentee might be able to share what you've learned.

1. Taking action:
    - What steps could your mentee take toward solving the problem the study addressed? (In other words, s/he should devise an action

plan that will be enacted in her/his classrooms over a period of time.)
- How could your mentee find out whether or not those steps are effective? (In other words, how could the action plan be assessed?)

2. Reporting results in a workshop or presentation: Some of the mentors whose projects we listed above reported results in a workshop to a larger group of mentees. Others, some in collaboration with their mentees, have given a presentation at a professional conference. How could you and your mentee report on the results of your project so that others can learn from it?
   - What's doable for your mentee? What would provide an appropriate challenge and also further encourage her/his professional development?
   - What audience would benefit most from what you've learned? How could you reach that audience?
   - What are some of the possible venues for a workshop or presentation? Would your institution or your mentee's welcome a workshop related to your project? What conferences are being held in your area that you and your mentee could attend?
   - What's feasible for you and your mentee? (Consider your schedules, proposal submission requirements and deadlines, conference/workshop dates, and potential for funding and being granted leave if necessary.)
   - How should you organize your workshop or presentation? (The Group Task Plan Template in Table 10.2 at the end of Chapter 10 will give you and your mentee some ideas about setup.)

3. Reporting results through publication: It has been said that "any sound study that is research-based deserves to be shared through publication."[10] This could include an article in a professional journal, either print or online, or a blog post or other online resource.
   - What are some of the publications that might be interested in your project? Start by looking at some of the articles in your resource folder. What journals do they come from? Does your mentee's institution have a blog or other resource you could write for, or is there a publication for your local TESOL organization?
   - What is doable for your mentee? What would provide an appropriate challenge and also further encourage her/his professional development?
   - What audience would benefit most from what you've learned? How could you reach that audience?

- What's feasible for you and your mentee? (Consider your schedules and submission requirements.)
- How would your article/post be organized? (For an article, see Table 11.3: Article Template in "Now It's Your Turn." This template could be used first to analyze some of the articles in your resource file and then as a step toward organizing yours.)

FACILITATING ACTION RESEARCH PROJECTS

We close with a reminder that the focus in this chapter is on using action research as a professional development tool. As a mentoring task whether one-on-one or with a group of mentees, a project is *facilitated* by you. Ideally, your mentees will shoulder increasing amounts of responsibility throughout the stages of the process. Most importantly, they should take ownership of the results by enacting and assessing change that benefits their students and inspires further cycles of action research, perhaps facilitated by them for another group of colleagues.

NOW IT'S YOUR TURN

If you are currently mentoring, the tasks below are designed for you. Alternatively, you could use them to consider an action research project you'd like to engage in with a future mentee. You could then write about your ideas in your mentoring journal or share them with your mentor support group.

Task 11.1: Resource Folder

Set up a resource folder that you and your mentee(s) contribute to as you find articles and other documents related to your action research project. This folder can be a hard copy or use an online file sharing system like Google Drive or Dropbox, or it could be a combination of both. (You could also ask a mentee to take responsibility for setting up and maintaining this shared folder.)

Task 11.2: Research Question/Hypothesis

Working through the following steps will help you and your mentee word your research question/hypothesis:

1. How do the authors of similar studies to the one you hope to do introduce their research? Two examples are below.
    - **Example 1:** *The purpose of this study is to extend previous research concerning the effect of drama-based instruction on L2 speaking to explicitly compare a drama-based approach with a traditional classroom. The study examines the extent to which learners improve along three dimensions of oral communication: fluency, comprehensibility, and accentedness. In addition, it evaluates the extent to which any measurable improvement extends across different speaking contexts. Our specific research questions are as follows:*
        1. *Do learners in a drama-based EFL program experience greater gains in oral fluency, comprehensibility, and accentedness compared to learners in a non-drama EFL program?*
        2. *Does their oral fluency differ across speaking tasks?"*[11]
    - **Example 2:** *[T]his study investigated the factors influencing teacher feedback on academic writing. In the study, we define teacher feedback as a teacher's written response toward a student's written work, with the aim of improving the student's performance (Van den Bergh, Ros, and Beijaard 2014). This working definition is sufficiently broad for any written response by the teacher to be regarded as feedback, including the use of symbols and short phrases. Specifically, the study sought answers to the following questions:*
        1. *Purpose of teacher feedback: what are the beliefs of the respondents regarding the purpose of feedback?*
        2. *Constraints on feedback practice: what constraints, if any, do the respondents face in their feedback practices?*[12]
2. What examples could you add from your resources?
3. Once you and your mentee(s) have compiled a list of examples, analyze them and make a list of potential prompts for introducing your study and wording your question/hypothesis. We've started your list below.
    - We are interested in identifying to what extent _____.
    - The aim of this research is to _____.
    - The purpose of this study is to _____.
    - What do _____ believe about _____?
    - Do (learners/teachers) _____?
4. Finally, what will your question/hypothesis be?

Task 11.3: Article Template

You and your mentee can use the article template in Table 11.3 below to analyze some of the articles in your resource folder so that you can use them as examples of research questions/hypotheses and data collection and analysis procedures. You could also use the template as a first step toward writing an article based on your action research project.

Table 11.3 Article Template

Title	*What is the title of the article?*
Abstract	*What summarizing information is included in the abstract (scope, purpose, study, results)?*
Introduction	*How is the article introduced? How is its main purpose stated?*
Literature Review	*What main points are made in the literature review?*
Research Questions or Hypothesis	*How is the research project introduced? What questions are listed, or what hypotheses are suggested?*
Research Methods	*How and from where was data collected? How was data analyzed?*
Results	*What did the study find? How are the results presented?*
Discussion	*What do the results mean, or what implications are described? What limitations or need for further study are listed? (When using this template to analyze articles, note anywhere your action research project might be able to fill the gap.)*
Conclusion	*What final points does the article end with?*

Task 11.4: Action Research Plan

Use the template in Table 11.4 below and the questions and guidelines in the chapter in order to plan an action research project with your mentee. Not every part of the plan can be completed before the project begins. Plan what you can now, and then add to it as you go. Also, feel free to adapt the template to better fit your situation.

Table 11.4 Action Research Plan Template

FRAMEWORK	
Setting: *Who will be involved in the project? How will you collaborate?*	
Outcomes/Essential Questions: *What outcomes will be reached or essential questions answered through the action research project?*	
Topic:	
Research Question/Hypothesis:	
Method:	
RESEARCHING	
Data Collection:	

	Data Sources/Investigation Procedures	Details (Where and When)	

Analysis:		

	Data	Analysis	

USING RESULTS	
Taking Action	
Action Plan	Assessment
Reporting Results	
Audience:	Potential Venues/Publications:

NOTES

1. Nancy Bell, *A Student's Guide to the MA TESOL* (London: Palgrave Macmillan, 2009), 96.
2. Jun Liu and Cynthia M. Berger, "TESOL as a Field of Study," in *TESOL: A Guide* (London: Bloomsbury, 2015), 98–101.
3. James Dean Brown and Theodore S. Rodgers, *Doing Second Language Research* (Oxford: Oxford University Press, 2002).
4. Zoltan Dörnyei, *Research Methods in Applied Linguistics* (Oxford: Oxford University Press, 2007).
5. Brian Paltridge and Aek Phakiti, eds., *Continuum Companion to Research Methods in Applied Linguistics* (London: Continuum, 2010).
6. Jim McKinley and Heath Rose, eds., *Doing Research in Applied Linguistics: Realities, Dilemmas and Solutions* (London: Routledge, 2017).
7. Gary Barkhuizen, Phil Benson, and Alice Chik, *Narrative Inquiry in Language Teaching and Learning Research* (New York: Routledge, 2014).
8. Gary Barkhuizen, ed., *Narrative Research in Applied Linguistics* (Cambridge: Cambridge University Press, 2013).
9. Thomas S. C. Farrell, *Reflective Language Teaching: From Research to Practice* (London: Continuum, 2007), 102.
10. Liu and Berger, *TESOL: A Guide*, 97.
11. Angelica Galante and Ron I. Thomson, "The Effectiveness of Drama as an Instructional Approach for the Development of Second Language Oral Fluency, Comprehensibility, and Accentedness," *TESOL Quarterly* 51, no. 1 (2017): 120, https:/doi.org/10.1002/tesq.290.
12. Hwee Hoon Lee, Alvin Ping Leong, and Geraldine Song, "Investigating Teacher Perceptions of Feedback," *ELT Journal* 71, no. 1 (2017): 61–62, https:/doi.org/10.1093/elt/ccw047.

REFERENCES

Barkhuizen, Gary, ed. *Narrative Research in Applied Linguistics*. Cambridge: Cambridge University Press, 2013.

Barkhuizen, Gary, Phil Benson, and Alice Chik. *Narrative Inquiry in Language Teaching and Learning Research*. New York: Routledge, 2014.

Bell, Nancy. *A Student's Guide to the MA TESOL*. London: Palgrave Macmillan, 2009. https:/doi.org/10.1057/9780230245105.

Brown, James Dean and Theodore S. Rodgers. *Doing Second Language Research*. Oxford: Oxford University Press, 2002.

Dörnyei, Zoltan. *Research Methods in Applied Linguistics*. Oxford: Oxford University Press, 2007.

Farrell, Thomas S. C. *Reflective Language Teaching: From Research to Practice*. London: Continuum, 2007.

Galante, Angelica and Ron I. Thomson. "The Effectiveness of Drama as an Instructional Approach for the Development of Second Language Oral Fluency, Comprehensibility, and Accentedness." *TESOL Quarterly* 51, no. 1 (2017): 1545–7249. https:/doi.org/10.1002/tesq.290.

Lee, Hwee Hoon, Alvin Ping Leong, and Geraldine Song. "Investigating Teacher Perceptions of Feedback." *ELT Journal* 71, no. 1 (2017): 60–68. https:/doi.org/10.1093/elt/ccw047.

Liu, Jun and Cynthia M. Berger. "TESOL as a Field of Study." In *TESOL: A Guide*, 97–178. London: Bloomsbury, 2015.

McKinley, Jim and Heath Rose, eds. *Doing Research in Applied Linguistics: Realities, Dilemmas and Solutions*. London: Routledge, 2017.

Paltridge, Brian and Aek Phakiti, eds. *Continuum Companion to Research Methods in Applied Linguistics*. London: Continuum, 2010.

Conclusion

In this book, we've come full circle. We started with you, the mentor. We talked about how you can engage in mentee-centered mentoring by building genuine relationships with your mentees and collaboratively identifying needs and setting goals for professional development. You learned about how to mentor in context with awareness of personal and cultural factors that influence your relationships with mentees and their classroom settings. With those factors in mind, you also developed some skills for interacting appropriately and aptly with them. Then, in the last section of the book, you began to make plans for specific tasks. As we conclude, we come back around to you, the mentor, and your professional development needs.

HERE'S WHAT HAPPENED: A MENTOR LOOKS BACK

At the end of her career—she'd recently retired, Penny looked back on her years in the profession of English language teaching. For much of her career, she'd supported the professional development of teachers new to the field. Her goal for these teachers, she explained, was to "wean" them from her direction and lead them toward "independent learning," all for the sake of their students.

For Penny, the mentoring process was reciprocal, not doing *for* the teacher but *with* them. "I respected them" and looked for what they could "bring to the table." Reflecting on a model (another colleague who had perhaps in some ways mentored her), she spoke of viewing mentees as a resource who helped her see classroom issues with "fresh eyes." Mentees, she mused, don't have all the experience that causes mentors to "forget what we know and make assumptions." Mentees become, for their mentors who have spent long years in the language classroom, "renewed eyes for tired teachers."

Penny also took this collaboration one step further by inviting feedback from her mentees. On one occasion, she asked the director of their program to lead a focus group with them and elicit feedback on her mentoring. The director then met one-on-one with Penny to pass on their ideas. At another time, she asked her mentees to craft a reference letter for her as if she were applying for a job as a mentor in another setting, and she admonished them, "You need to put something negative in here." During our conversation, she pulled their letters out of her files and used them as evidence of what she'd learned.

PROFESSIONAL DEVELOPMENT FOR MENTORS

Penny's reflections on her career are a reminder to look forward. What stood out in our conversation was how she aimed toward independent learning. Early in this book, we said that the ultimate goal of the mentoring process is self-evaluation and autonomy. That's what Penny was working toward with her teachers. She was also journeying toward her own independent learning of mentoring. She inspires us to add, as we conclude this book, that the ultimate goal of your journey is this—to take ownership of your professional development as a mentor.

Throughout this book we've attempted to support your professional development and to mentor you, the reader. We hope that by reading and interacting with this book, you've grown in your role. We hope that the "What Do You Think?" and "Now It's Your Turn" sections have encouraged you toward the deeper levels of Bloom's Taxonomy for Mentoring: analyzing and evaluating what you've read, applying some of our ideas and then reformulating them (the templates, for example) into your own, and also regulating some of your decisions based on your values and those of your mentees.

NOW IT'S YOUR TURN

We have attempted to support your professional development. Now, how can you support your own? What's your next step? Perhaps a few of the tasks below will resonate with you and bridge the gap from book to ownership. But then, it's your turn.

Task c.1: Mentoring Journal or Mentor Support Group

At the beginning of the book we suggested that you process ideas in a journal or in regular conversations with other mentors whether face-to-face or virtually. Both are tools you can continue to use. Or, you can begin to use either now. See the Preface, Tasks p.1 and p.2 for more information. Some of the other ideas listed here are topics or tasks you can begin with for your journal or support group.

Task c.2: Philosophy of Mentoring

Also at the beginning of the book, we said that by the end you should be able to articulate your philosophy of mentoring. This could include the following sections:

1. Mentee-Centered Mentoring
2. Mentoring in Context
3. Interactive Mentoring
4. Task-Based Mentoring.

You could also include a description of your individual mentoring style supported by a rationale based on both theories and experiences (yours and those of other mentors). Don't forget also to consider your values and how your beliefs about learning, teaching, and mentoring influence your philosophy.

Task c.3: Feedback

Penny's creative efforts to invite feedback from her mentees have inspired us. How could you invite feedback on your mentoring? Could you ask your mentees to write a reference letter as Penny asked hers? Who could you invite to be your mentor and offer you feedback on your mentoring?

Task c.4: Observation

Ask someone to observe one of your mentoring encounters (either face-to-face or virtually). Feel free to use or adapt the observation form in Table c.1 below. (We've already adapted it from an observation form in Chapter 9.) Invite your mentor (from Task c.3) to observe you facilitating a mentoring encounter (perhaps leading a post-observation discussion or one of the tasks from Section IV). Alternatively, you could set up peer observations with your mentor support group or record a mentoring encounter and use the form for self-observation.

Task c.5: Action Research Project

With another mentor (perhaps one or two from your mentor support group) collaboratively identify and solve a mentoring problem through inquiry. Follow the steps in Chapter 11 to choose a topic, formulate a question, collect and analyze data, and take action based on what you learn. Then, consider publishing your project.

Task c.6: Workshop on Mentoring

Some of our mentors have given workshops on mentoring. Usually the audience includes managers or administrators who are responsible for supporting the professional development of teachers within their purview. Imagine the possibilities for personal growth when you lead others away from supervision and encourage them to develop mentoring skills. Consider an audience and a topic (potentially from your action research project) for a workshop on mentoring. Use some of the ideas in Chapter 10 to help you plan and then facilitate the workshop.

Table c.1 **The Story of a Mentoring Encounter**

\multicolumn{3}{l}{Write the "story" of what happens during the mentoring encounter as you observe (a summary of events, including any apt quotes from mentor or mentee). In the left column, keep track of the time as events in the story unfold. In the right column, list questions you might ask in your follow-up conversation with the mentor.}
Time	Events in the story	Questions

About the Authors

Since 1993, **Melissa K. Smith** has lived more years in China than in her home country of the United States. Currently, she runs Li Ai Education Consulting Company, which equips teachers, encourages students, offers resources to schools, and inspires others to participate in education relief work in remote areas. She also teaches pre-service and in-service English language teachers in the School of Foreign Languages at Ningxia University.

Marilyn Lewis has taught English and other languages in New Zealand, Britain, India, and Cambodia. Since her retirement as Senior Lecturer at The University of Auckland, she continues to organize workshops for teachers of English in various parts of the world. Her other interest is in writing (especially co-writing) books, articles, and book reviews.

Index

action research projects 165–167, 186; article template 179, **179**; case studies 169–170; completing at a distance 172–173; facilitating 166, 177; framework of plan 173–174; hypothesis 177–178; narrative research 171; outcomes of mentoring course **166**; plan 173–177; plan template **180–181**; program evaluation 171–172; purpose of 167; researching 174–175; research question 177–178; research synthesis 172; survey research 170; types of research 168–169; using results 175–177
administrators, needs assessment of 29
advisor 4
affect 29, 32, 41, 45, 62, 130; outcome of mentoring course **166**
affective filter 86; cathartic mentoring style 103; factors influencing 86–87; group mentoring 155; mentoring 92–93
affect sphere 25
article template 179, **179**
Art of Crossing Cultures The (Storti) 65, 76
autonomous learning 92
awareness: beliefs and values 78–79; context resources 80; cultural 71–72; developing self- 80–81; of differences 73–77; interwoven challenges 76–77, 79; pedagogy 78, **80**; of self 77–79; sorting the layers 75–76; teacher-student relationships 78, **80**; teacher support group in China 74; training teachers in civil war 72–73, 73–74

beliefs, awareness of 78–79, **80**
benchmarks: classroom context **26**; contexts 24; exercise in negotiating 24–26, 34; framework **25**; terms 24; types of needs 24–26
bilingual learner identity 43
blog, interactive mentoring 90–91
Bloom's taxonomy: for mentoring *89*; questions *113*
body language 129
buy-in, term 11

catalytic mentoring style 102
cathartic mentoring style 101–102
Centre for the Canadian Language Benchmarks 75
China: teacher support group in 74; teaching methodology course in 42
Chinese education: researching 65–66; tensions in proverbs 60–64; understanding differences 75–76
civil war, training teachers in 72–73, 73–74
classroom context 57–58; benchmarks **26**; classroom dynamics for mentors

59–67; culture comparison 68–69; interview 68; mentoring in 58–59, *59*, 67; researching the 64–67; resources 69; teaching 58–59, *59*; tensions in 60–64

classroom observation: assessing learning **147**; assessing learning by self-observation **148**; being catalytic 131–132; characteristics of 132, 134–137; being collaborative 130–131; data collection 135–136; designing an observation form 140–141, **143**, 185; devising an approach 140; disappearing 132; focused *vs* open-ended 134–135; forms and notes 134; management of start-up issues 129–132; managing errors **145**; mentor's attention 136; plan for 137–140, **141–142**; signposting 132; being supportive 129–130; teachers reflecting on being observed 128; teacher *vs* student talk time **144**; timing 135; tracking student attention **146**; virtual 137

Classroom Observation Tasks (Wajnryb) 134
coach 4
collaboration: classroom management 130–131; collaborative dialog for group mentoring 155–156
co-mentoring 60–61
Common Core State Standards Initiative 75
Common European Framework of Reference for Languages 75
communication: balancing mentor and mentee interaction 88–90, 93; convenience in 98; conversation openers **104**; face-to-face *vs* virtual interactions 90–92; interaction analysis 107–109, **108**; modes of 96–99; politeness 98–99; *see also* feedback
competencies term 23
confronting mentoring style 101
conversation openers **104**
co-teaching 60–61
critical friend, term 7

cross-cultural mentoring, needs analysis in 33
cultural awareness, defining 71–72

directive to facilitative continuum, feedback 99, *99*, **108**
distance mentoring: completing projects at a distance 172–173; in Middle East 27; modes of communication 96–97; needs analysis in 32–33
dynamics, definition 58

eliciting, classroom management 131–132
empowerment 39
encouragement, classroom management 129–130
English program, mentoring in intensive 30–31
essential questions: mentoring 43–45; outcomes or 46–47; reframing outcomes as 43–44

feedback 95, 185; convenience in 98; conversation openers **104**; directive to facilitative continuum 99, *99*; for facilitative mentoring 107; group mentoring 155–156; interaction analysis 107–109, **108**; intervention framework 99–101, *100*; meeting needs through 101–103; message *105*, 106; modes of communication 96–99; pragmatics for 103–107, *105*, 109; reaching goals through 101–103; register and rules of politeness 98–99; relationship *105*, 106; situation *105*, 106–107; types of 99–101; *see also* communication

Geography of Thought, The (Nisbett) 87
Goals, reaching through feedback 101–103
group mentoring: advantages and disadvantages of 154–156; affective filter 155; collaborative groups 158; group task plan 158–160, 162, **162–163**; mentoring proposal 162; mentoring relationship

154–155; one-way transmission *vs* collaborative dialog 155–156; peer observation form **163**; setting 161; settings 156–157; teacher support groups 152–153, 158; virtual group settings 157–158; workshops 150–152, 157–158
growth mindset: encouraging a **121–122**; fixed *vs* **119**, **121–122**

Hofstede, Geert 67, 76

informative mentoring style 101
inside track 21
interactive mentoring 90–91
intervention framework, feedback 99–101, *100*, **108**

knowledge 25, 41, 130; outcome of mentoring course **166**

learner ownership: scale *48*; taking 47–48; term 39
learning: autonomous 92; taking ownership of 47–48; Zone of Proximal Development (ZPD) 85–86
learning assessment **147**; self-observation **148**
life cycle teacher 22, *22*

mentees: attitudes of 11; exercise in negotiating benchmarks 24–26; expectations of 11; identifying 16, 19; needs assessment of 28–29; personal characteristics of 10–11
mentor 4; advisor 7; attention in classroom observations 136; classroom dynamics for 59–67; classroom management for 129–132; cross-cultural perspectives on 12–13; definition of 4–5; experienced teacher 7; expert teacher 7; feedback 95, 185; identity of 10; interpersonal communicator 7–8; looking back 183–184; mentees of 10–11; model 8; needs assessment of 29–30; professional development for 184; qualities of good 5–9; relationship 4–5; responsibilities of 8–9; roles of 6–8; supervisor *vs* 4; support group 185; *see also* classroom observation
mentoring: attitudes towards **11**; balancing input and output 103; from benchmarks to outcomes 41–45; Bloom's taxonomy for *89*; classroom context of 58–59, *59*, 67; complexity of 79; cross-cultural relationship 12–13; distance, in Middle East 27; encouraging a growth mindset **121–122**; essential questions 43–45; feedback for facilitative 107; fixed vs. growth mindsets **119**; in intensive English program 30–31; interactive 90–91; mentee-centered 3; online relationship 13–14; organization of relationship 14–15; outcomes 41–42; philosophy of 185; self-assessing styles 101–102; setting up plan for 45–46; story of encounter **186**; tasks in organization of 15–19; ultimate goal of 39–41
mentoring contract 16, 17, 47
mentoring journal 185
mentoring plan: examples **49**, **50–51**; setting up 45–46, 47; template **48**
metaphors, teacher support group 74
Middle East, distance mentoring in 27

needs assessment 28–30; administrators 29; cross-cultural mentoring 33; distance mentoring 32–33; getting started on analysis 32–33; mentee 28–29; mentors 29–30; negotiating benchmarks in 24–26, 34; plan 34–35; as reference tool 32; students of teachers 29; supervisors 29; terms for 34; tools for 33; whole person needs 32

observation *see* classroom observation
online relationship: complications and possibilities for *14*; mentoring 13–14
organization, mentoring relationship 14–15

INDEX

outcomes: essential questions or 46–47; mentoring 41–42; mentoring course **166**; reframing as essential questions 43–44

pedagogy 78, **80**
politeness, register and rules of 98–99
prescriptive mentoring style 101
professional development for mentors 184
proverbs: for teachers 68; teaching Chinese 60–64
purpose statement 16, 17, 18

questions: analysis **115**; Bloom's taxonomy for mentoring *113*; defend their honor technique 118; encouraging a growth mindset **121–122**; funnel technique 117–118; importance of 112; intentions of 114–116; prompts 120–121; questioning for reflection and autonomy 119–120; questioning techniques 116–119, 121; scaffold technique 116; springboard technique 118; types of 112–116; variety 113–114

research: case studies 169–170; classroom context 64–67; hypothesis 177–178; narrative 171; program evaluation 171–172; qualitative and quantitative **169**; survey 170; synthesis 172; types of 168–169; *see also* action research projects

self: awareness of 77–79; developing self-awareness **80**, 80–81
self-assessing mentoring styles 101–102
settings: advantages and disadvantages of group 161; group mentoring 156–157, 161; virtual 157–158
signposting, classroom management 132
skills 25, 41, 130; outcome of mentoring course **166**

Skype 33, 96, 97, 137, 158, 170
SMART (Specific, Measurable Attainable Reasonable and Time-limited) outcomes 41-42
standards term 23
strategic investment 39
students needs assessment of 29
supervisor 4; mentor *vs* 4; needs assessment of 29
support group 185
supportive mentoring style 102

teacher: life cycle of 22, *22*; reflection on being observed 128; standards for 22–23; support group 152–153, 158; training in a civil war 72–73, 73–74; *see also* classroom observation
teaching: classroom context of 58–59, *59*; methodology course in China 42
TED Talk 158
TESOL (Teaching English to Speakers of Other Languages) International Association 22, 23, 58, 60, 67, 89, 167
timing, classroom observations 135

values 26, 29, 32, 41, 45, 62, 130; awareness of 78–79, **80**
Values in English Language Teaching (Johnston) 26
virtual group settings 157–158
virtual observations 137
VoIP (Voice over Internet Protocol) 137

WeChat 96, 97, 109n3
whole person needs 32
workshops 150–152, 157–158, 186

Zone of Proximal Development (ZPD) 85–86, 111, 130; autonomous learning 92; balancing input and output 88–90, 93

 Taylor & Francis eBooks

Helping you to choose the right eBooks for your Library

Add Routledge titles to your library's digital collection today. Taylor and Francis ebooks contains over 50,000 titles in the Humanities, Social Sciences, Behavioural Sciences, Built Environment and Law.

Choose from a range of subject packages or create your own!

Benefits for you

» Free MARC records
» COUNTER-compliant usage statistics
» Flexible purchase and pricing options
» All titles DRM-free.

Benefits for your user

» Off-site, anytime access via Athens or referring URL
» Print or copy pages or chapters
» Full content search
» Bookmark, highlight and annotate text
» Access to thousands of pages of quality research at the click of a button.

REQUEST YOUR FREE INSTITUTIONAL TRIAL TODAY

Free Trials Available
We offer free trials to qualifying academic, corporate and government customers.

eCollections – Choose from over 30 subject eCollections, including:

Archaeology	Language Learning
Architecture	Law
Asian Studies	Literature
Business & Management	Media & Communication
Classical Studies	Middle East Studies
Construction	Music
Creative & Media Arts	Philosophy
Criminology & Criminal Justice	Planning
Economics	Politics
Education	Psychology & Mental Health
Energy	Religion
Engineering	Security
English Language & Linguistics	Social Work
Environment & Sustainability	Sociology
Geography	Sport
Health Studies	Theatre & Performance
History	Tourism, Hospitality & Events

For more information, pricing enquiries or to order a free trial, please contact your local sales team:
www.tandfebooks.com/page/sales

 | The home of Routledge books | **www.tandfebooks.com**